CONTENTS

	Introduction	*v*
CHAPTER 1	Why take a year out?	*1*
CHAPTER 2	Planning and surviving your year out	*7*
CHAPTER 3	Organised gap year schemes	*22*
CHAPTER 4	Working abroad	*35*
CHAPTER 5	Voluntary and community work in the UK	*60*
CHAPTER 6	Voluntary and community work abroad	*84*
CHAPTER 7	Travel and holidays in the UK	*119*
CHAPTER 8	Travel and holidays abroad	*129*
CHAPTER 9	Courses and work experience in the UK	*138*
CHAPTER 10	Courses abroad	*150*
CHAPTER 11	Challenges and expeditions	*164*
CHAPTER 12	Now it's over. . . .	*179*
	Further reading	*184*
	Some useful websites	*187*
	Useful addresses	*188*

For
gap year students everywhere

INTRODUCTION

Taking a year out is an exciting and challenging opportunity. It is a choice not to be made lightly, but the rewards for doing it can be great.

How you choose to spend your year out is very important. Whether you are thinking of taking a year out at 16+, after the sixth form, or after college or university, it may be the only opportunity you get to spend a year doing exactly what you want to do! To make the most of the year, you need to choose an activity that is right for *you*. But you also need the practical information which will help you get your year organised. This book will help you do this.

The opportunities for spending your year out – 'the gap year' – are many and varied. You may decide to do voluntary work, paid work, study, travel, take a holiday or even do nothing at all – although the latter choice is likely to leave you bored!

It can be an investment in the future. In the current economic climate, students have to work harder and may enter the world of work without the all-important 'people' skills that so many employers look for in today's market. If nothing else, a year off mixing with a wide range of other people and having to adapt to different ways of working and living will be an invaluable addition to your academic qualifications and practical skills – although these too can be added to in a gap year.

Because gap year opportunities cover so many different themes, trying to find your way though that maze and make a sensible decision about your year out is very hard. This book helps to make that choice easier by providing you with everything you need to know in order to make a decision about *whether* to take a year out, and then how to spend it. The book takes you through the things you need to consider before taking a year out, and gives you the basic practical information you need for whatever choice you make. It describes the different major types of gap year opportunities available and tells you what you need to know about each type of project.

Each chapter has a detailed address list which gives full information about each organisation concerned and any specific qualifications, skills or criteria you must fulfil. Finally, there is an extensive booklist to help you find out more about anything in this book that interests you.

Many of the opportunities described in the book cannot be neatly compartmentalised under specific headings. I have therefore made my own judgement about which chapters they should go in, or put them in the chapter which seems nearest to their own description of what they do. Bear in mind that many organisations arrange several different types of schemes. I have mentioned this where applicable and cross-referenced between chapters where relevant. It is worth looking in several related chapters to see whether other organisations with a slightly different main purpose also offer opportunities that might interest you.

You will notice that I have not included a chapter on finding paid employment in the UK. That is because *you* are the best person to look for jobs in your local papers or the Jobcentre. You can contact local businesses in your local *Yellow Pages* or *Thomsons* or ask family, friends and other contacts what jobs might be available. Don't forget to try places like hospitals, zoos, leisure centres or holiday centres. Contact local groups of national organisations or charities to see if they offer paid temporary work for all or part of your gap year. There are, however, some organisations such as The Year in Industry or the Army Gap Year Commission that offer specific gap year employment opportunities and are included in chapter 9.

This book is an ideas book as much as a practical manual. Read through it or dip into it. Contact the organisations which seem of interest and then plan your year. Use the basic information section to help you make your preparations – then set off on your gap year in a positive frame of mind.

You may only get this one opportunity to take a year off and do what *you* want to do. This book will help you do it.

> **Note:** the fact that an organisation is mentioned in this book does not imply endorsement by the author or publishers, nor devalues organisations which have not been mentioned. Organisations are listed alphabetically within each chapter and all addresses are provided at the end of the book. Regard all costs and prices as approximate and contact the organisation you are interested in for their up-to-date details.

Cost guide

£ = budget activity: free or costs under £100
££ = costs £100–£500
£££ = costs £500–£1000
££££ = costs £1000–£2000
£££££ = costs over £2000

WHY TAKE A YEAR OUT ?

You have opened this book because you are thinking of taking a year out, a 'gap year'. The thought of taking a year out to do what *you* want is enticing. Fun, freedom, adventure, perhaps even money seem to be on offer for a year. So why not go for it?

A year out can provide all of these things. But before you make a firm decision, take some time to think about whether a year out is really what you want. If it is, then make sure you know what you want to do with it. A year with nothing planned can be depressing and a waste of time. You need to take a positive attitude if you are to benefit. You need to start preparing for it well before the time comes to take the plunge. Read this chapter to help you find out *why* you want to take a year out. Knowing why you want to do it will help you choose activities that will enhance the experience.

Advantages of a year out

Most universities and employers look favourably on gap year applicants if they have shown good reasons for taking a year out and have not just drifted into it. They value the maturity, confidence, social and other skills a gap year can bring. But they agree that applicants who cannot give a good reason for the year out are viewed with some suspicion. *'Broadening my mind through travel'* may be an acceptable reason; *'Because I felt like it'* may not. So before you contemplate a year out, be clear in your own mind *why* you want to do it and what advantages you think it will offer. Be prepared to explain these in detail at university or job interviews. Make the reasons clear on your application forms too.

Colleges find that gap year students tend to be more mature and motivated. They mix better with their fellow students and work harder because they have a better idea of where they want to go. They also contribute more to college life in general, because they are used to being a part of a team, either at work or study.

Employers also look kindly on former gap year students. They want employees who are experienced and mature and can deal better with the unexpected, who are better team workers and have better 'people' skills and are better mixers in general. If their gap year has also equipped them with skills which other applicants may not have, such as a better grasp of a foreign language, then that too is a plus.

From a personal development point of view, a gap year may be a good idea. If you need money, lack experience of mixing and working with other people, have led a sheltered life between school and home, then a year out may give you the chance to expand your experiences and mature. Just dealing with a whole year of life on your own can boost your self-esteem and confidence.

Your family may well have mixed feelings. On the one hand they will be proud of your independence; on the other, there will be worries about your safety, health and future prospects. They may also worry that you will be a different person when you return and that you will grow apart from them. This may all be mingled with a little envy!

You will need to reassure them. Do this by being clear about what you want to do and why, by involving them in your plans and preparations, and by making sure that you have taken as much precaution as possible against ill health and danger. This book will help you with these preparations.

You might like to contact The Year Out Group (see Useful Addresses). The Year Out Group publishes a set of guidelines to help young people, their parents and advisors to select appropriate opportunities and placements.

Why *not* to take a gap year

There may be practical reasons for not taking a year out. In some subjects, such as maths, it can be difficult to keep up with a subject after taking such a long break. In those departments, universities and colleges prefer students straight from school. Music is another subject where deferment is not usually encouraged, and music colleges which do occasionally allow it can insist that students re-audition. Check with your prospective university and the subject director about whether there would be any practical problems about taking a year out.

You might also want to get qualifications as soon as possible, or have limited opportunities for a gap year. In that case there is no point in delaying entry to higher education. Whatever you do, don't take a year out unless you have a plan of action. Otherwise you could end up wasting your time and possibly extending your time out indefinitely.

Why do you want a year out?

If you know what you want to do and why, a year out can be worthwhile and exciting. So why do you want to take a year out? Make a list of reasons. Is it for any of the following?

- to experience life and/or work before three more years of education?
- to make money?
- to study a relevant subject in a new situation?
- to sample one or more careers before making a final choice?
- to add to your skills?
- to extend personal experience?
- to fill in time constructively?
- to challenge yourself?
- to make friends?
- to travel?

There are as many reasons for taking a year off as there are students who want to take them. It does not matter if your reasons are not the same as those of your friends. The important thing is to be clear in your own mind what you want to get out of the time. When you have made your list, put your reasons in order of priority. So if meeting people is more important to you than learning a new skill, you will start looking for an activity that will bring you into contact with lots of other people rather than a study course with small classes. Let's look at the reasons listed above in a bit more detail.

To experience life/work before three more years of education

It is quite natural to want to do something a little different with your life at this point. You have spent a long time in education. You want to extend yourself and find out what different experiences life has to offer before you settle down to several more years of learning. This can be an exciting and fulfilling time, but bear in mind that a gap year is not suitable for everyone. If it will mean not getting into the college or course that you want or foregoing other important experiences, then you will have to weigh up whether it is worth it.

To make money

Going to university is expensive and few students can manage without some kind of additional income to supplement their loans. The more you can save beforehand, the better. Or you may want to save some money in order to take part in a gap scheme that would otherwise be too expensive. Or you might just want to experience work and to have some spare money to spend for the first time.

Don't forget that what you earn will have to cover living expenses too. Even if you live at home while you are working, you should contribute to household expenses. So bear this in mind when calculating how much you will be able to save.

Remember that if you are taking paid employment in the UK, other than pocket money for voluntary work, and earn over £84 a week, you will have national insurance contributions deducted from your pay as well as tax. But if you earn less than the single person's allowance per year (£4385 in 2000–01) you can claim the tax back at the end of the tax year. If you are working during school or university holidays, ask your employer to give you a form P38S. This allows you, as a student, to be exempt from tax if you don't expect to earn more than your personal allowance during the tax year. If you are working during your gap year, and so are not yet studying full-time, ask for P46. Do not try to avoid paying what you should. When you leave each job, ask for a P45 to pass to your next employer.

To study a relevant subject in a new situation

Do you want to learn a new subject away from the pressures of exams, a subject you have chosen? The obvious example of this is studying a foreign language in that country. But you can also study other subjects in a new situation – art/literature/music could all be studied abroad to great benefit or in the UK away from home. Any subject studied in a new place with new people is stimulating and motivating and will help improve your skill in that subject.

You will also meet people with a similar interest to you, which gives you a talking point and is a good way of making friends. This is particularly important if you are studying abroad.

To sample careers

You may know now what career you are hoping to do, but be unsure whether it is really right for you. Do you want to use a gap year to try out the skills needed for the job, or even the job itself, before you start your training? Doing that will either confirm your interest in that job or it could point the way to new interests. It can give you the chance to earn and learn and develop contacts for later. This could be the best time to get a mentor, a professional in your chosen work, to help and encourage you. It also gives you the opportunity to network, to build up friends and colleagues whom you will stay in touch with when you do start work. Trying a job before you go to university or college will give you a good basis on which to develop your career at college. You will know better what you want to do and where you want to go with your future.

To add to skills

You may want or need to learn new skills – either out of interest or for your university course or eventual career. It might be a condition of year out employment that you acquire a particular skill before you start. Typical skills might be word processing, keyboard, shorthand, language, study skills or any kind of practical skill. You might want to use the time to get an extra A or AS level or a certificate in a particular subject. Now is the time to do so.

You could spend your whole year learning a new skill or take a short course during the year. Whether you aim for a qualification or not, acquiring a new skill will be worthwhile.

To extend personal experiences

Have you always wanted to find out about archaeology or scuba diving? If you have a particular interest that you would like to pursue, a year out could provide the opportunity. There are plenty of classes or intensive short courses in practically any subject you care to mention. There are also courses if you need to retake an A-level or take a new one.

To fill time constructively

Do you have to take a year out because of personal circumstances or because you will be taking exams later than usual? In that case you need to find a way of using the year constructively so that it is not wasted. If nothing else, this could be the time to earn some money.

It might be tempting to let the fact that you *have* to take a year out be an excuse for doing nothing much. But you would find this dissatisfying and it would certainly not impress a university or employer. Turn your circumstances to your advantage by doing something constructive.

To challenge yourself

Has your life been uneventful or sedentary so far? Then you might want to stretch yourself intellectually or physically and to experience danger, excitement, expectation, and stimulation.

By testing yourself and finding out what you are capable of, you expand your horizons and increase your confidence. As you face challenges, you learn to cope with what life offers.

To make friends

Do you want to meet people? Make new friends? If you think you don't make friends easily, then putting yourself in a situation where you have to mix with other people in a new environment can be very helpful. This also applies if you want to meet different kinds of people if, for example, you come from a single-sex or religious school. 'People' skills are in demand in any kind of job nowadays, so it is a valuable experience. Also, you may just want to make more friends!

Don't assume that everyone is more confident and knows more than you. In a new situation most people want to get on with other participants. You may be nervous about arriving on your own and talking to new people, but you will soon find that time flies past as you all help each other.

To travel

Do you want to spend your gap year experiencing new countries and cultures? This is probably the usual reason for taking a year out. It is particularly stimulating if you have never travelled much before and/or never been abroad. It is also useful if you want to improve your foreign language skills.

Whether you want to travel alone or with friends, you will meet new people and see new places. If you are nervous about arranging your own travel, you can go on an organised trip with a travel company or take part in an organised project abroad. That way you will have the travel experience with the support of other people, as well as doing something worthwhile.

Checklist

1 Find out from your local authority when and how to apply for a student loan (or discuss finances with your parents if they will be paying).
2 Check with the university whether they prefer continuous attendance from school to college for your subject.
3 Decide what kind of gap year experience you want.
4 Check on the organisation you will be dealing with.
5 Book up early.
6 Involve your parents in preparations and plans.

2

PLANNING AND SURVIVING YOUR YEAR OUT

You will waste your year out unless you organise carefully and work out a timetable based on your needs and expectations for the year. You need to decide what you want to do, how much time you want to spend doing it, and which activities are the most important to you, so that you can prioritise them. You should also make a list of everything you need to do before your year out starts. The most important of these is making arrangements for when you return.

Deferring a year

Before you embark on a year out, you must sort out your university or college place for the year after. If you are taking a year out after college and before employment, then contact your future employer, if relevant, to make arrangements for a deferred start.

You can specify a deferred year of admission on your UCAS form, but must give reasons for it. If your university or college accepts your deferred status:

▶ contact your college to confirm your place and check the starting dates;

▶ if you will be unable to collect your results yourself, get someone else to do so or arrange for your school to post them to you;

▶ if someone else is collecting your results get them to contact you to tell you what they are;

▶ make sure you have emergency phone numbers for your school

7

and college in case you need to talk to them about last-minute problems;

▶ if you have a part time job, give notice in good time;

▶ ask someone at your home to deal with any emergencies for you;

▶ give one of your parents permission to open any official-looking mail addressed to you, in case it needs a response quickly;

▶ make sure you tell your family how they can contact you if you will be travelling;

▶ book tickets in advance, unless this is being arranged for you, and check departure and arrival times.

Contingency plan

You should have a contingency plan in case the year does not go as you had hoped. Have you planned other activities in case your original plans fall through? Have you decided what to do if you change your mind about the course you will be taking next year? Think about these things before you start.

How much time have you got?

You probably expect to take a whole year out. But your circumstances may not be typical. Perhaps you have to retake exams, for example. In which case you will not have a whole year of time. Work out how much time you expect to be able to take out, so that you can decide what activities you can reasonably fit into the time available.

One year is the maximum amount of time it is usual to take out, and many gap year opportunities in this book do last that long. Others, also intended for year out students, last for less time – perhaps from one or two months or more – and can be done as part of your year out experience. You may want or need to combine several of these in order to complete your year. For example, you may want to earn some money for part of the year in order to go travelling, or you might need to gain some relevant experience or qualification before taking up a longer-term project. Take a look at how long each organisation expects you to commit yourself for, and apply in good time, so that you can arrange the options to fit in with your plans.

Remember that you may need to start earning money or learn new skills up to a year or more before you start your year, so don't leave decisions about what to do and where to go until the last minute.

Deciding what to do

You may already have a gap year project in mind. If not, use the information in this book as well as the reading list at the end to help you decide. Then turn back to this chapter to help you plan your year.

Write down everything you would like to do during your year out, and then list them in order of importance. Work out how much time you can spend on each one and how much they will cost you, and then make a timetable for the year – including time beforehand for raising money and learning necessary skills. Choose carefully, because if you choose a scheme lasting for a year, that is a long time to be stuck doing something you find you hate!

To help you decide what you want to do, and whether you want to do it at home or abroad, consider the following:

- gap year scheme
- voluntary or community work
- expedition or challenge
- paid work
- travel or holiday
- study or training course.

Before you commit yourself to any occupation for your year out, make careful checks of the employer or organisation you will be dealing with. Ask these questions:

1 Does this organisation have a good reputation?
2 How long has it been operating?
3 Can it show me any references or can I speak to people who have used this organisation before?
4 How much will it cost?
5 What will be provided – accommodation, travel, expenses?
6 If I will be working, will I be trained?
7 Will any training cost me?
8 Are applicants insured while on the scheme?
9 Will the organisation deal with the necessary paperwork?
10 Will the organisation send people to check on my progress and monitor the scheme?
11 What happens if I fall ill or hate what I am doing?
12 Will the organisation liaise regularly with my parents about my health and safety?
13 How much preparation does the organisation provide?
14 Are there any contingency plans for an emergency?

Use the information in this book to make an initial choice. Write, phone or E-mail for information and then ask the questions above. Only when you are satisfied should you commit yourself to the scheme. Remember that some of the choices get booked up as much as 18 months in advance, so make contact as soon as possible.

Raising the money

Work out a basic budget for your year out beforehand. Add up all the money you have got, or hope to get, from your own savings, relatives and friends, borrowing or earnings. Then work out what you are likely to spend. Estimate your living expenses, travel costs, payments for training or placements and allow some for a holiday if you are taking one. By subtracting one from the other you can see how much money you need to raise before you go.

If the money from those sources will not be enough, consider raising money through sponsorship. Use one of the guides to sponsorship in the booklist or write to local firms asking for help towards your trip. Keep your letter short but give enough detail for them to judge its merits. Explain why you want to go and stress the benefits to the organisation. Tell them what you can offer in return for sponsorship – perhaps wearing a branded T-shirt or supplying photographs of you using their equipment. Promise (and deliver) a full report of the trip or experience afterwards.

If you are going to be working on a volunteer project abroad, the organisation arranging it will usually give you help and advice about raising money before you go. Sometimes they have grants available, so it is worth asking them.

Some organisations do give grants to individuals if it is for a good cause, so read one of the books on the subject, such as *The Directory of Grantmaking Trusts*, to find out how to apply.

Getting ready to go

Depending on where you will be going and what you will be doing, you will need to think about:

▶ passports/visas	▶ clothing	▶ red tape
▶ tickets	▶ luggage	▶ companions
▶ insurance	▶ Customs	▶ special needs
▶ money	▶ languages	▶ health.
▶ accommodation		

Allow time for applying and getting accepted on a scheme or job, if that is what you want to do. Some gap year schemes ask you to apply up to 18 months in advance because of the waiting lists.

Before you start applying for work, travel or study anywhere, get lots of passport-sized photographs. You will need them for application forms, passport, CVs, travel cards, student ID cards and so on. If you are going abroad, take a few spare photographs with you in case you need them for any official purpose. And keep one or two photocopies of the key documents, just in case.

Youth and student cards

Cards especially for young people or students give you discounted travel and in some countries admit you to public attractions such as museums or art galleries free or at a reduced rate. Sometimes you need to show your UK card to a representative in the country concerned to get a discount card which is valid for that country.

ISIC (International Student Identity Card)

This student card is the only internationally recognised proof of student identification, and is accepted in over 90 countries worldwide. In cooperation with the International Student Travel Confederation, ISIC has negotiated special rates with all the major ferry, airline and overland travel operators. You can expect to get about 30 per cent off normal prices. These offers are only available through authorised ISIC agents, so check before booking. The card also admits you at reduced rate to many attractions in the UK and abroad.

The card is available in the UK to all students over the age of 12 in full-time education, including those students taking a gap year and who have secured a place at university. To apply for an ISIC card get an application form from your student union or from a local ISIC issuing office (see Useful Addresses). Complete it and return it with £6, a passport-size photo and some proof of full-time student status such as your NUS card or a letter from your school or college. Some student unions may be able to supply the card to you directly with the appropriate documents and information about where to get discounted travel and other benefits. With the card you get a handbook that gives details of a major selection of international discounts and information about services such as Helpline.

Passports and visas

You must have a full passport before you travel abroad and it must be valid beyond the date of your return. If you have no passport or it needs renewing, get a form from your main post office, large travel agent or passport office and complete it. Send it to the passport office recommended on the form. You can get your application checked at the post office for a small fee and sent securely to the passport office. Applications sent this way are given priority treatment. Allow one month if possible. If you need a passport quickly you can get one by taking the form to the office in person, but even then you should allow 48 hours. If you apply in person there is an additional fee. If you will need lots of visas in your passport, make sure that there are plenty of spare pages left.

Unless a company is arranging your visas, if you need them, you will need to get a work or visitors visa. In Europe you will not normally need a work permit. For each country requiring a visa, you must obtain one in advance unless it has been made clear that you can get one at the airport on arrival in the country. In that case you will need to take the necessary money. If you are getting your visas yourself, allow at least three months or use a visa service – ask at a travel agent. You *can* go to the embassies in person, but some of them have short and erratic opening hours. You will do better to arrange your travel through one of the travel companies mentioned in chapter 8. They have experience of obtaining visas. Check also whether you will need anything else, such as money for an entry or exit tax payable at the airport or border.

Tickets

The further in advance you can buy your tickets, the cheaper they will be. So as soon as you know where you are going and how you want to get there, contact one of the travel agencies (see chapter 8) and book them. If you are travelling with an organisation, they will usually arrange your tickets for you.

Insurance

If you are travelling abroad, make sure you have accident, health and baggage insurance. This may be included in any travel arrangements but, if not, buy your own. It is especially important to get health insurance if you will be travelling to any country that does not have reciprocal health arrangements with the UK covered by form E111 (see Health, below). If you will be driving outside the UK, make sure you are covered by the relevant insurance.

Money

Take some local cash. In the UK you can use any branch of your bank or building society and a credit or bank card is useful. When going abroad take a certain amount in foreign currency but then use a card where possible. Although common European currencies are sometimes available immediately, it can take a week or more to order money or travellers cheques from a bank, post office or building society. Ask for smaller denominations than are usually supplied. If necessary, you can get money sent to you virtually anywhere. The high street branches of Thomas Cook, for example, can arrange transfer of money abroad very quickly.

Budget for living expenses, including board and lodging, before you go. Be realistic, but try to keep to a set amount each day. If you spend all your money in the first week, you will be in trouble. If your expenses are paid for beforehand, allow some money for pocket money.

Accommodation

Organised schemes will normally arrange your accommodation. If you have to arrange your own, try to do so in advance by booking through a student travel agent. Otherwise contact the tourist information office when you arrive to find temporary accommodation. You could also use Youth Hostels – join the Youth Hostels Association (YHA) – but you usually need to book in advance. Membership of the YHA automatically gives you membership of the International YHA, so you can use it to stay in youth hostels overseas. Other cheap lodgings may be obtained by looking at rooms to share on college noticeboards. For one-day stops, ask the local tourist information board.

In the UK, camping is also cheap, but again you often need to book in advance. Many UK campsites do not accept groups of young men only – so travel in a mixed group.

When abroad, the International YHA is a good option, as is camping – you can usually just turn up. If you are staying in hotels or bed and breakfast, try to arrange accommodation beforehand.

Clothing

Most people take far too much clothing with them when they travel. Take the absolute minimum for your needs. Buy anything extra at your destination as you need it, or get clothes sent from home. Be aware of cultural and religious differences if travelling abroad and dress accordingly. Women should not wear skimpy clothes or swimwear in countries where this is unacceptable. Not only is it offensive but you will attract undesirable attention from men. Women might want to take a long skirt as well as a long-sleeved, high-necked shirt if travelling in Muslim counties. A hat or headscarf is useful both for keeping off the sun and visiting religious buildings.

Luggage

Wherever you go, remember that you have got to carry your luggage, so do not pack anything you won't need. Try to keep to one rucksack and one small hand-held bag to keep with you. Use a bum-bag, money belt or neck purse for carrying money, passport, etc. Don't try to take everything with you, like backpackers who appear to carry their whole house on their back. Follow the experienced traveller's rule – set out on your bed what you need to take and then reduce it by half. Roll clothes to reduce creases and pack more in.

What to take

The following is a useful basic list of what to take:

- two T-shirts
- long-sleeved shirt
- jumper
- jeans
- skirt
- jacket
- pyjamas (or use T-shirt and shorts)
- shorts
- swim costume
- spare socks and underwear
- hat/headscarf
- insect repellent
- medicines/glasses
- money/credit card
- student card
- wash things
- towel
- writing things, diary, address book.

If you are going abroad, take the above plus:

- passport, visas, insurance documents
- tickets
- doctor's letter about any medicines
- foreign cash or traveller's cheques
- map/guidebook
- sunblock cream
- sunglasses
- money belt/bum-bag/ neck purse.

Customs

You must have a valid passport available, and can go through the green channel at UK Customs if you have nothing to declare. Do not exceed the maximum limits for duty free or duty paid goods. These limits are prominently displayed at all ports and airports or look on the HM Customs & Excise website for details (see Useful Addresses). Customs officers have the right to search your baggage if they suspect you are carrying prohibited goods such as drugs. Cooperate with Customs if you are asked to open your baggage.

Never carry or take any drugs abroad. Drug taking is illegal virtually everywhere and in some places can result in imprisonment or worse. Always pack your own bags and never carry anything through Customs for *anyone*, not even your best friend. Don't leave your luggage unattended. If you are stopped and asked to submit to a body search, then you should be told why. At the time there is nothing you can do except submit. But if it is unjustified, make a note of the officer's name and complain to their superior at the time and in writing immediately you get home.

Languages

Try to learn some of the language of any country you are visiting before you get there. Even a few simple phrases and *'please'* and *'thank you'* go down well. You can learn through classes, tapes, books, radio, TV, or school and college.

Don't be afraid of sounding silly when you try to speak a foreign language. Most people are pleased that you are making the effort, and in any case it is only courteous to do so. You will be surprised how quickly you pick up a few simple words and phrases.

Red tape

Every country has its own red tape – rules and regulations. The main thing is to be as organised as possible before you go. Plan well in advance and take an emergency number with you, and the number of the nearest British Embassy or Consulate. Be patient too. If things seem to take a long time, don't panic. In some countries bureaucracy takes longer than in others.

Companions

You may like to travel with friends; or perhaps you prefer to go alone. If you want to go with other people, have a short trial run beforehand. If you argue all the time, then at least you can make other arrangements for your main trip. It would be awful to be stuck with people you couldn't stand for months at a time.

If you do fall out with friends half way through a year, then either come to a compromise and carry on, or go your separate ways if this can be done safely.

Before you go, work out how you will be sharing things such as the costs of the trip. Think about such things as who will be responsible for making travel arrangements and booking accommodation. Will you all be driving? If so, for how long at a time and how often? If you are travelling around, who will decide where to go and when?

If you haven't got someone to travel with, there are organisations that can introduce you to possible travelling partners, for a fee. Try *Travel Companions*. You can also look in the small ads of magazines and newspapers for people of the same age advertising for travelling partners. If intending to travel with someone you don't know, find out as much about them as possible. Introduce them to your parents and make sure you leave details of your intended route.

Special needs

Most of the organisations in this book will accept students with special needs. However, some cannot because the nature of the activity does not permit it. For example, in some cases students with physical disabilities may find it difficult to take part because of the mobility demands of the activity. If you have special needs, explain them clearly to the employer or organisation at the start so that they can accommodate you where possible and help you play a full part.

Disability is no bar to travelling the world – read *Nothing Ventured: Disabled People Travel the World*, published by Rough Guides.

Health in the UK

If you are staying in the UK but will be away from home, make sure if you need glasses that you take a spare pair. If you wear disposable contact lenses, arrange to collect them from another branch of your home optician. If you need regular medication, take your repeat prescription with you, as well as ample supplies. Remember that you can go to any doctor and ask to be seen as a temporary patient if you are away from home for up to three months. If you are ill and it is an emergency, any doctor can be called out to see you. You can also call NHS Direct for advice (see Useful Addresses).

Get your teeth checked before you leave. If you need emergency dental treatment, try a local dentist. If they cannot see you, go to the accident and emergency department at the local hospital. Some hospitals have a dental school which will treat patients needing emergency dental treatment.

Health abroad

If you will be spending your year abroad, get a free copy of the booklet *Health Advice for Travellers* from your post office. As well as useful information, it contains an E111 form. Fill it in and the post office will stamp it and you can then obtain free or reciprocal health treatment abroad in countries which are part of the scheme. Take the form and a photocopy with you, as in some countries both are required if you need treatment. If so, the original will usually be returned to you. The accompanying booklet tells you how to claim money back for health treatment. Usually you will need to pay up-front and then reclaim afterwards, so take a credit card if you can.

Most European countries in the European Economic Area (EEA), plus Iceland, Liechtenstein and Norway, give free or reduced treatment with the E111. Details about the specific countries are in the booklet. More than forty other countries also provide reciprocal treatment and emergency medical treatment. The rest of the world – over 100 countries – has no healthcare agreements, so you will need to take out full medical insurance to stay in one of those countries. It is advisable to take out medical insurance in any case, wherever you go.

Visit the Department of Health website for up-to-date health advice for travellers.

Medicines

When going abroad, take enough of your usual medicine to see you through. Take it in prescription containers or with a doctor's note so that Customs and police don't think you're using some dangerous drug. Check that any medicinal drug you have been prescribed is permitted in the country you are going to. If not, see whether your doctor can prescribe an acceptable alternative. If you do have any medical condition, take a written record of it with you. Have a dental check before you go.

See your doctor at least two months before you depart to find out what vaccinations you will need and when to get them. For some diseases you must allow longer – immunisation against Hepatitis B, for example, can take six months to give full protection. You can also go to a travel health clinic. The Hospital for Tropical Diseases Travel Clinic Helpline or MASTA can also tell you what vaccinations you need (see Useful Addresses). At a Tesco 'Traveller' pharmacy you can get a free computer printout giving details of the risks of the country you are visiting.

You should try to get your vaccinations well in advance, but if you do leave it late you can try an airport travel clinic (British Airways has 28 travel clinics in the UK – use the BA phone number in Useful Addresses to find their locations) or Medicentre at London's Victoria station. They will charge for the service and should generally not be used as an alternative to your GP.

Malaria

While you are seeing your doctor about vaccinations, check whether you need protection from malaria in the countries you are visiting. You can also phone the Hospital for Tropical Diseases Travel Clinic Helpline, Malaria Healthline, or MASTA. All these are premium lines. Take the malaria treatment advised before, after and during your time abroad.

Treatment is usually available from a chemist and should be taken for a week beforehand, throughout your stay, and a month afterwards. Cover yourself up, use mosquito nets and cream too.

Basic health

Follow these basic health rules wherever you go:

- wash your hands before and after going to the toilet and handling food;
- when in doubt about the water, drink bottled water;
- avoid uncooked food unless you peel or shell it;
- don't eat food that has been exposed to flies;
- only eat ice-cream from a shop or café;
- be careful about eating shellfish or fish.

Sun

If you travel abroad you will probably be exposed to the sun much more than in the UK. Skin cancer is on the increase, so stay out of the midday sun for at least two hours and use a high factor sunblock and apply it after every swim. Keep your arms and legs covered and wear a hat or head scarf in very hot sun.

Rabies

Rabies is still active abroad, so do not touch even tame animals. This applies even to seemingly safe areas outside the UK such as Europe and North America. Rabies is usually fatal. If you are bitten by any animal, get immediate treatment and report it to the police. You usually only need rabies vaccine before travel if you are likely to be exposed to unusual risk of infection or will be making a long journey in remote areas where medical treatment may not be immediately available. Even if immunised, you must seek treatment urgently if bitten by an infected animal.

HIV/AIDS

This is a risk wherever you are. The answer is not to have casual sex and if you do have sex *always* use a condom. Do not inject non-prescribed drugs and do not have your skin pierced abroad. Only have essential dental or medical treatment.

If you have any doubts about the medical facilities which are likely to be available, take your own *emergency sterile medical equipment pack*, available from larger pharmacies and via the British Airways travel clinics. The pack includes a variety of syringes and needles, sutures, etc, and a Customs declaration.

Political risks

If there is any doubt about whether the political situation in any country will be dangerous for travellers, consult the Foreign & Commonwealth Office (FCO) for travel advice.

Safety

Be as aware of safety everywhere as much as you are at home. Just because you are away from home does not mean that you can disregard sensible personal safety rules. Don't walk alone in back streets after dark. Don't wear conspicuous jewellery. Do use a money belt. Don't leave your passport with anyone else and don't go away with strangers.

In touch with home

Your family will be worried, however supportive and encouraging they were before you left. Send regular letters – take some addressed envelopes and paper so all you need to do is write the letter and get a stamp. Send post-cards – try to communicate once a week if you are abroad so that everyone knows where you have been and that you are well. Dial home direct – make a note of the countries number prefix for calling the UK.

If you will be travelling, letters can be sent to the town or city next on your route for you to collect on arrival. It is therefore important to leave a timetable for your travels with your family, and to tell them if you vary your plans. Letters should be marked with your name, surname in capital letters and underlined, and *Post Restante,* and can be sent to the Central Post Office of any town or city you will be visiting, for you to collect. Letters are kept for two to four weeks and you might have to pay a fee when you collect your mail.

Homesickness

It is not a sign of weakness to feel homesick, nor unusual. Keeping in touch with home will help. Keep busy and try to make friends and it will get better. If you are on an organised scheme, contact the representative to see if they can help. If you really can't bear it, then go home, but try to do that only if you must. Sometimes it is better to give up and try something else, but you should give it a good try first.

A year out on a budget

You do not have to be rich to take a year out. Even the schemes which cost a lot can be paid for by raising sponsorship money or working during your spare time. Many are free or cheap. Generally surviving your year with little money is perfectly possible if you plan ahead.

Pay for as much as you can before you go and take a credit card with you. If you are travelling abroad with friends, change all the group's money together to save on bank charges. Buy things where the locals do, and shop and eat where they do. Whether in the UK or abroad, keep away from tourist areas, especially shops and restaurants, which are often more expensive. Eat one main meal a day and don't spend money on expensive snacks – local bread and cheese is healthy and tasty.

You don't need a lot of expensive clothes – unless you are dealing with the public you can manage with a couple of T-shirts, a long-sleeved shirt, jeans, a jumper and a jacket (see the list above).

If you need specialist equipment, hire or borrow it. You may have friends who can lend you a tent or a ski jacket, for example. If travelling in a group, see if you can share things like a camera or guidebook.

Make the most of the free sights every place has to offer. If in the countryside, walk, swim (where safe) or visit or stay with friends and relatives where possible. In a city, find free or cheap art galleries and museums (use your student card), local cinemas, cheap cafés, parks, riversides, etc. Play sports with new friends. Look out for pavement art shows, or student cafés.

Travel is often cheaper if you travel early or late in the year. Travel in good weather where possible, as it saves wear and tear on your clothes as well as your temper. Use your student card to get cheaper travel tickets, use rover tickets or weekly, monthly or yearly passes. If you are going to be travelling to many countries, then a round-the-world ticket will work out cheaper and be more flexible than separate tickets. Use the country's specialist cheap transport, such as the USA's Greyhound buses. If you are flying, book off-peak flights, use a charter flight or book an unusual route. Travel companies such as those in chapter 8 can advise you about the cheapest way to travel. For cheaper rail travel, book in advance and use your student railcard. Get a tourist or discount pass in the country you visit and use the Eurorail and other discount schemes. Long-distance road travel is cheapest by coach. Book at the last minute, buy a return ticket which is usually cheaper than two singles, and use non-express coaches. Cycling is also cheap and you can buy a second-hand bike or borrow or rent one. Plan a route so that you don't cycle more miles in a day then you can comfortably manage (test yourself before you go!). Insure your bike against accident or theft.

Budget accommodation depends on the country you are going to. Consult tourist offices and guides and use any relevant discount cards. Check universities and colleges for advertisements for rooms to let. The further out from the centre of a town you are, the cheaper it will be. Some foreign hotels charge by the room not the person, so if you are with friends it can be cheaper to share. Camping is cheap, but don't camp away from official sites if you can help it because it is frowned upon in some countries.

Some countries provide temporary student accommodation in cities in the summer, so ask at the local tourist office. If you are travelling a lot, then going by overnight train can save money if you don't pay for a sleeper. Live cheaply by doing an activity which gives you board and lodging and a little pocket money, or take some paid work or find live-in work, such as hotel work. You can try asking farmers if you can camp in their field or use a barn or shed to sleep in. Don't sleep rough if you can help it; it is illegal or disapproved of in some countries, and can be dangerous. You can try sitting around in railway stations looking as if you are waiting for a train. But in some countries officials will check up on you if you look as if you are trying to go to sleep – so stay awake and keep your feet off the seats.

One of the best ways of surviving cheaply, whether at home or abroad, is to ask fellow travellers or local people for advice about where to eat, live and be entertained cheaply. Take a notebook and make a note of their advice. Pass it on to others in your turn.

Checklist

1 Check the arrangements for starting at university or work before you leave.
2 Arrange contingency and emergency plans.
3 Make a timetable for your gap year – an unplanned year is likely to be wasted.
4 Work out your budget well beforehand, so that you know how much money you need to find before you go.
5 Arrange passport, visas, travel tickets, insurance well in advance.
6 Make sure your health needs can be catered for.
7 Don't take more than you need.
8 Pay for as much as you can before your go.
9 Look for budget ways of spending your year.
10 Ask other travellers and local people for advice about cheap ways to live.

ORGANISED GAP YEAR SCHEMES

One of the best ways of getting your gap year organised is to apply to an organisation that can arrange it for you. There are many organisations which have developed schemes especially for gap year students.

Gap year organisations arrange projects which vary from voluntary work to expeditions, from teaching English as a foreign language to environmental projects. The projects differ in length from a few weeks to a whole year, but they all have one thing in common: either they cater specifically for gap year students or they claim that their projects are suitable for a gap year.

The advantages of using one of these organisations is that they arrange everything for you – work or expedition placement, insurance, visas, flights, accommodation and training if necessary. You have the backing of an experienced organisation and are drawing on their wealth of expertise. They have been running such schemes for a number of years and have arranged projects for thousands of students and so have a great deal of knowledge of the pitfalls and joys of taking part. They also have representatives in the countries concerned who check on projects and can give help if there is an emergency. This means that parents and schools have confidence in these schemes and are more likely to feel happy about your participation.

On the other hand, although these schemes usually involve voluntary work, the cost of taking part can run into thousands of pounds. Not only do you pay an administrative fee to the organisation, but you need to pay for insurance, air travel, and possibly training. You are expected to provide this money yourself through sponsorship or by other means. You do get help with fundraising, but the onus is on you to raise the money in time, which can be difficult. Projects which do pay you only provide pocket money. Another irritation is that some of the organisations only have a limited number of places available, and as they are also very popular you may need to apply to some of them as much as eighteen months ahead.

As long as you are the right age, live in the UK, have a UK passport and speak good English, you will be eligible for these schemes. Normally you need to be in good health but people with physical disabilities can usually be catered for. However, young people with learning difficulties may have to look elsewhere for their gap year experience. Gap year organisations do look for other qualities as well and many have an interview and selection process. It is a good idea to contact your preferred schemes well in advance to see if you will qualify.

You do need to have the right attitude to your proposed project. If you simply want a holiday for a year, you are not likely to be selected. Community work in a foreign country or an expedition to a far-flung part of the world, for example, is likely to be demanding. You also need the ability to cope with unusual situations and to deal with problems. With the best will in the world, projects do not always go smoothly and you may not always be able to get hold of the project representative, so you need to be adaptable and not easily upset. You need to be able to get on with all kinds of people, some of whom will not speak English. Whatever you do, you will be living and working with strangers, so somebody who is withdrawn and uncooperative will not be welcome. Some projects also require specific skills, for example ability in a foreign language, so check with the organisation of your choice before you apply.

The organisations listed below cater specifically for the gap year or they state that their projects are particularly suitable for gap year applicants.

££££ | Africa & Asia Venture

Africa & Asia Venture is an organisation which enables students to gain work experience (unpaid) with youth in Africa, Northern India and Nepal. Students are placed in selected secondary and primary schools teaching a variety of subjects. There are also opportunities for conservation work in Kenya working in wildlife management or on cultural projects, both lasting three months. There are then three weeks in which to backpack before going on safari to areas of interest and outstanding beauty in the chosen country.

HOW LONG IT WILL LAST
Approximately three months plus three weeks' backpacking.

WHERE YOU WILL GO
Kenya, Tanzania, Uganda, Malawi, Zimbabwe, India or Nepal.

PAYMENT
The work is voluntary (unpaid).

THE COST TO YOU
Approximately £2190 to cover careful selection and placement, comprehensive health and personal effects insurance, an orientation course on arrival and in-country back-up, living allowance and accommodation, an

all-inclusive safari and a donation towards educating a deserving child or the purchase of school equipment. You will also need to find the air fare to Nairobi, Harare, Delhi or Kathmandu, entry visas and extra spending money. You will get advice about raising funds.

WHO CAN APPLY
A-level students going on to further education or undergraduates considering taking time out can apply. You must be 17 or over and enjoy working with young people or in conservation.

WHEN AND HOW TO APPLY
Contact Africa & Asia Venture at the address given as early as possible, informing them when you are leaving school or university.

SELECTION PROCESS
You must complete an application form and attend an interview to be assessed on your suitability.

PLACEMENT
You will be placed in a school or project according to your skills, strengths and personality.

TRAINING
On arrival volunteers are given a four-day orientation course. This will be held in scenic locations. Topics covered will include health and welfare, teaching skills, security, safe travel, conservation and local language.

SUPPORT FOR PARTICIPANTS
Special emphasis is placed on in-country back-up. In each country there are representatives to provide on-the-spot support and advice. You will be covered by a comprehensive medical policy and a local expert will provide emergency cover.

£££-££££
GAP Activity Projects Ltd (GAP)

This is an educational charity that offers voluntary work opportunities overseas for young people in their year out between school and higher education, training or employment. The work offered includes assisting with English language teaching; conservation work; helping with general activities in schools; caring for the disadvantaged; outdoor education and farming.

HOW LONG IT WILL LAST
Four to eleven (average six) months.

WHERE YOU WILL GO
The scheme operates in Argentina, Australia, Brazil, Canada, Chile, China, Czech Republic, Ecuador, Falklands, Fiji and the South Pacific, Germany, Hong Kong, Hungary, India, Israel, Japan, Jordan, Lesotho,

Malaysia, Mexico, Nepal, New Zealand, Paraguay, Poland, Romania, Russia, Slovakia, South Africa, Swaziland, Tanzania, USA, Vietnam and Zambia.

PAYMENT
You will get free board and lodging and usually pocket money.

THE COST TO YOU
The cost can vary depending on the destination. The costs (based on current prices) include a non-refundable registration fee of £35, GAP's fee of £515 which is payable two months before departure, insurance (£68–£160) and, if you decide to teach English as a foreign language, about £130 for a one-week teaching skills course. On top of this, add your travel costs and budget for any subsequent travel.

WHO CAN APPLY
You must be aged 17 (turning 18 by the start of your placement) and hold a British passport.

WHEN AND HOW TO APPLY
Contact GAP for a brochure/application form. Apply as early as possible in your final A-level year. Interviews take place from mid-October and run until all the places are filled up. So the earlier you apply, the better your chances will be. The registration fee of £35 is payable on application.

SELECTION CRITERIA
GAP interviews all applicants but not everyone is successful. This is because some placements need certain skills such as a knowledge of a foreign language or sporting ability. The skills required will depend on which country you choose, and are explained in detail in the GAP brochure. In general, GAP looks for people who are lively, interested, outgoing, resilient and adaptable, and who can cope with some discomfort, boredom and loneliness. A sense of humour is essential.

PLACEMENT
Consideration is given to the needs of the overseas host as well as the student looking for a job. You are encouraged to be as flexible as possible about your choice of placement in case you cannot be offered the one you prefer. The interview is a 'matching' meeting where GAP matches you to an opportunity.

TRAINING
Any student wishing to teach English as a foreign language must take the teaching skills course. Every project has a briefing and orientation session.

SUPPORT FOR PARTICIPANTS
There are representatives in the host country to help you, and GAP's Project Managers (based in the UK) visit their placements at least once a year. GAP's UK headquarters also run a 'seven days a week' emergency telephone service.

£££££ | Project Trust

Project Trust sends school leavers to live and work overseas as volunteers for twelve months from August or September. It offers the following categories of project: English language assistants in schools, colleges and universities; care work in homes with deprived, disabled or homeless children; assisting in health and community projects in hospitals or with aid organisations; educational projects, including teaching in primary and secondary schools and assisting with extracurricular activities; environmental and development projects; and outdoor activity projects in Outward Bound schools.

HOW LONG IT WILL LAST
Twelve months.

WHERE YOU WILL GO
The current programme includes projects in Africa, the Far East, the Middle East, Central America and South America and the Caribbean.

PAYMENT
The host organisation or Project Trust will pay you a living allowance.

THE COST TO YOU
The average cost of sending a volunteer is about £3350, which works out about £280 per month. Project Trust raises an additional £500 itself. Project Trust provides fund-raising advice and also workshops around the country in order to assist people to raise the money. This money covers selection, training, airfares, insurance, support and debriefing.

WHO CAN APPLY
You must be between 17 and 19 at the time of going overseas and in full-time education with a view to obtaining higher education qualifications. You must be in good health and have a British, Irish or Dutch passport as well as have determination, energy, enthusiasm and initiative.

WHEN AND HOW TO APPLY
Applicants need to send a registration fee of £10 with a completed application form and four photos. Applications are accepted from March to November of the year before you wish to go. Exact dates for application and an application form are available from Project Trust. Address enquiries to the Director.

SELECTION PROCESS
Candidates are initially interviewed in their local area and are then invited to a four-day selection course at the Trust's headquarters on the Isle of Coll. Project Trust offers places overseas to about 80 per cent of these candidates.

PLACEMENT
The final choice of country and project is based on a volunteer's prefer-

ence, strengths and skills and the kind of work the candidate is best suited to.

TRAINING
All volunteers attend a week's briefing course at the Project's purpose-built selection training centre on the Isle of Coll in July and early August. The course covers information on the prospective country, type of work, medical advice, equipment needed, guidance on cultural and physical adjustments, getting visas and guidelines on how to get the most out of the year. It also includes the training most necessary to your needs.

SUPPORT FOR PARTICIPANTS
A local representative oversees the projects and visits all projects in the country during the year to give support to volunteers. Volunteers are also visited by a member of Project Trust's UK staff who keep close contact with the volunteer throughout the year, as well as acting as a contact point for their parents. In emergencies the local host, the in-country represen-tative and the UK country desk officer will deal with the problem. The organisation provides personal accident insurance and will arrange medical flights if necessary.

£££-£££££ | Quest Overseas

Quest Overseas arrange the combination of Spanish language courses, rewarding voluntary work projects (children's projects and conservation projects) and challenging expeditions to South America. For example, you could spend three weeks in Ecuador learning or improving your Spanish with individual tutors, then look after children in Peru for six weeks and finally learn to lead a six-week expedition through Chile, Bolivia and Peru. Alternatively you could spend seven months in Paraguay combining Spanish lessons in the afternoons with looking after children in the morn-ings, followed by the six-week expedition through Chile, Bolivia and Peru.

HOW LONG IT WILL LAST
Three months, but with the option of a further three months of indepen-dent travel.

WHERE YOU WILL GO
South America.

PAYMENT
None.

THE COST TO YOU
'Quest South America' costs £3050 excluding direct donations to UK Registered Charities with whom Quest Overseas work, international air fares and insurance. You will need some pocket money

WHO CAN APPLY
Gap year students.

WHEN AND HOW TO APPLY
Write or telephone Quest Overseas for an application form (no application fee). Applications are considered 3–18 months in advance of January, February, March and April departures.

SELECTION PROCESS
This is by interview followed by team meetings for successful applicants.

PLACEMENT
A specific choice of project in South America is discussed at interview.

TRAINING
Pre-departure Preparation and Expedition Training Weekend.

SUPPORT FOR PARTICIPANTS
Full-time Support for participants is provided by Quest Overseas staff and their representatives.

£££-£££££ | Raleigh International

This organisation is a charity which gives young people the chance to carry out demanding environmental and community projects in the UK and remote parts of the world. Participants rotate between three activities: community work, conservation and adventure.

HOW LONG IT WILL LAST
Most expeditions last ten weeks and there is at least one starting most months between January and October.

WHERE YOU WILL GO
The destination countries vary from year to year. As an example, the 1999 expeditions were to Namibia, Chile, Belize, Mongolia, Ghana and Oman. In 2000, expeditions were to the same countries, except that Brunei replaced Oman.

PAYMENT
No payment – you do it for the experience.

THE COST TO YOU
You will need to raise between £600 and £3200 in sponsorship money. This includes all transport and insurance costs. In addition, you might pay a registration fee of (currently) £5 and the cost of a selection weekend of £20. Raleigh International provides support for fundraising and runs events in which people can participate. Many companies send employees as part of a training programme and there are some grants available from Training Enterprise Councils, local authorities and charitable trusts. Economically disadvantaged candidates may be allowed to pay less.

WHO CAN APPLY
You can apply if you are aged between 17 and 25, can swim 500 metres and speak English. You must be physically capable of looking after your-

self. If you are over 25 you could join an expedition as a volunteer staff member.

WHEN AND HOW TO APPLY
Send an A4 envelope to Raleigh International for information about expedition dates and an application form. Apply at least six months before the starting date of the expedition you wish to join. Or visit the Raleigh International site website and apply online.

SELECTION CRITERIA
You will be invited on an introductory weekend to check your suitability for going on an expedition. You do not need any special skills, but Raleigh are looking for people who are motivated, enthusiastic, adaptable and who can work in a team. You will also need to show leadership ability and a commitment to others, as well as have a sense of humour. In addition, 200 places are available each year through a Youth Development Programme for young people from disadvantaged backgrounds.

PLACEMENT
You decide which expedition you would like to join and apply for it.

TRAINING
Participants are expected to learn the necessary skills during the expedition. Young people on the Youth Development Programme get a week's special pre-expedition training and two weekends.

SUPPORT FOR PARTICIPANTS
Volunteer staff accompany each expedition.

££££ | The Right Hand Trust

The Right Hand Trust provides a chance for Christian young people to work and live in Africa helping a rural community. The work is in Anglican parishes, although missioners come from all denominations. The work may include teaching, leading sports, pastoral care, administration, recreational and vocational work and will involve participation in public worship and bible study.

HOW LONG IT WILL LAST
Eight months.

WHERE YOU WILL GO
Africa. Recent placements have included Uganda, Kenya, Zimbabwe, Swaziland, Malawi, the Windward Islands, The Gambia, St Helena, Namibia and Zambia.

PAYMENT
The work is voluntary.

THE COST TO YOU
About £2300, which covers training, flights, accommodation, etc.

WHO CAN APPLY
You must be a Christian between the ages of 18 and 30 and have the backing of your home church and preferably communicant status within it. You should be willing to adapt to the lower standards of living and different customs of your host community.

WHEN AND HOW TO APPLY
Apply to The Right Hand Trust well before the introductory course in July.

SELECTION PROCESS
Selection is at the discretion of The Right Hand Trust.

PLACEMENT
You can choose placements from the parishes on offer for the Challenge.

TRAINING
You attend a three-day introductory course in July and attend a brief meeting in September with people recently returned from Africa and the West Indies. During September to December you receive training and orientation and make sponsorship contacts with the Trust's assistance. Also in December you receive a cross-cultural course in Birmingham with the USPG (United Society for the Propagation of the Gospel). You travel to Africa in the first week of January and have a few days' acclimatisation before taking up a development post which will continue until after Easter. In April you get two weeks' travel in-country or to neighbouring locations to widen your experience of the region and continue your development work from May until August. During August or September you return to the UK and take part in a debriefing, exchange of development experiences and report back to your sponsors.

SUPPORT FOR PARTICIPANTS
You receive support from The Right Hand Trust, the overseas partners and other volunteers.

£££-£££££ | Schools Partnership Worldwide (SPW)

This organisation arranges teaching placements and environmental programmes for young people.

HOW LONG IT WILL LAST
The placements last from four to nine months.

WHERE YOU WILL GO
Nepal, Tanzania, Zimbabwe, Namibia, Uganda, India and South Africa.

PAYMENT
None.

THE COST TO YOU
The basic cost of a placement is from £2200 to £2500 plus the costs of small-scale practical learning activities and spending money.

WHO CAN APPLY
You must be between 18 and 25. Apply as early as possible in the academic year before your year out. Contact SPW and they will send you an information pack and application form.

WHEN AND HOW TO APPLY
Obtain information about how to apply from the Director.

SELECTION PROCESS
You will be selected on the basis of your application form, personal statement, references and performance at an assessment weekend. You will be advised of any further procedures.

PLACEMENT
Volunteers can choose their countries and types of programme, provided there are places available. The actual placement in the country is usually decided when volunteers have arrived overseas. Volunteers often have a say in this, but ultimately it is up to the field officer.

TRAINING
Before departure there are regular briefings, and background reading is recommended. You also receive intensive in-country training lasting four to seven weeks.

SUPPORT FOR PARTICIPANTS
SPW has its own field staff in the country working from a permanent office. They check out projects, arrange in-country training, organise accommodation and subsistence payments and visit volunteers in their placements. For mutual support, teachers are posted in pairs to schools within easy reach of each other. Members of staff travel with the environmental groups. During the outreach sessions staff remain in close contact with the SPWs, who work in groups of 6–8. On arrival, all SPWs are briefed about emergency contact procedures.

St David's (Africa) Trust

This organisation arranges projects in Ghana, Mali and Morocco working with disadvantaged young people. In the country you visit you will be a guest of a major national organisation for the young. There are also equine healthcare projects in Mali and Morocco working with the Society for the Protection of Animals Abroad (www.spana.org.uk), a British animal healthcare registered charity.

HOW LONG IT WILL LAST
The projects last three months from September or six months from January each year.

WHERE YOU WILL GO
Ghana, Mali and Morocco. There are plans to include Senegal and Sierra Leone from about 2004.

PAYMENT
None.

THE COST TO YOU
Prices for 2000/2001 are £1500 for three months and £2500 for six months.

WHO CAN APPLY
Anyone aged 18–25 can apply. For projects in Mali you need A-level French.

WHEN AND HOW TO APPLY
Apply at any time. Complete the online registration form or get one from the Trust's office.

SELECTION PROCESS
If the Trust likes your application you will be asked for a reference. If the reference is acceptable you will be called for an interview. You must be available for interview in London or Wales.

PLACEMENT
Placement is made after acceptance.

TRAINING
You will be sent written information and attend London pre-departure briefings and meetings with former volunteers. You will receive two weeks of in-country language, culture and street-cred lectures given by resident European volunteers and retained nationals.

SUPPORT FOR PARTICIPANTS
There are scholarships and grants available. You receive 24-hour SOS support. In the country you are visiting, resident European and national project leaders will meet you at least weekly to review your project and codes of practice.

£££££ | World Challenge Expeditions

This organisation organises overseas adventure education programmes for young people. One specifically for gap students is Gap Challenge. The placements are abroad and professionally organised. A mixture of paid and voluntary positions is offered – for example, working on a conservation project, teaching in a secondary school, or hotel work – although most positions are unpaid. The fees include a 12-month return tickets so that after completing their placement students can travel independently for six months either in the same country or further afield. Departures are annually in September and January.

HOW LONG IT WILL LAST
The placements are from three to six months, plus six months for travel.

WHERE YOU WILL GO
Australia, Belize, Canada, Costa Rica, Ecuador, India, Malawi, Malaysia, Nepal, New Zealand, Peru, South Africa, Tanzania, Zanzibar.

PAYMENT
Most placements are for voluntary work. Some paid placements are available, but pay is basic.

THE COST TO YOU
The total cost of a placement is from £1567 to £2887 depending on the country and placement and includes a 12-month return flight, airport to workplace transfer fees, first night's accommodation, in-country administration, UK administration, and World Challenge placement fee. There is an additional application fee of £50. You must also pay for insurance and visas. Food and accommodation is usually extra. The cost of induction courses may or may not be included, depending on the placement.

WHO CAN APPLY
You must be 18 but under 25 by the time you depart for your work placement, as well as self-motivated and self-reliant. You will need a full UK passport and visas for the relevant countries. Work permits are required for Australia and Canada, and Canada also requires evidence of your acceptance on a full-time university or college course on your return to the UK.

WHEN AND HOW TO APPLY
Complete an application form and return it to World Challenge with four passport photos, a character reference from your school or employer and the application fee. You will then be invited to a Gap Challenge induction course.

SELECTION PROCESS
Selection is an informal procedure carried out over two days, when you will be interviewed and assessed in group activities by experienced group leaders. You will be briefed on work placement opportunities and fundraising and get the chance to talk to recent Gap Challenge volunteers. There is no quota system and every student has an equal chance of acceptance.

PLACEMENT
Applicants can specify the country they wish to travel to and a placement is found for them.

TRAINING
You attend a Skills Training Course lasting two or three days during which you are given relevant basic training to prepare you for your placement. You also receive on-site advice and support from Gap Challenge in-country representatives once you reach your destination.

SUPPORT FOR PARTICIPANTS

Gap Challenge representatives meet students at the airport and take them to their work placements. They live near student work placements and will check on students' progress. Representatives are available in case of emergencies, and World Challenge staff are in regular contact with the representatives.

WORKING ABROAD

You have three choices if you want to work abroad during your gap year. You can look for work yourself, arrange work through an agency, or take work through one of the specialist organisations such as those for au-pairs, couriers, or kibbutzim.

The type of work available will depend on which of these three options you choose, as well as your own interests and skills. If you look for work yourself, whether beforehand or after you arrive abroad, you are likely to be given temporary short-term work such as washing up, waitressing, fruit picking, teaching English, etc. If you use an agency or organisation, you will have access to a wider range of jobs. If you use a specialist organisation, you will know exactly what kind of work you will be doing – there is no excuse for not understanding what an au-pair does, for example.

In order to work in most countries you will need to be 18 or older, although a very few countries will sometimes accept au-pairs of 17. Make sure you know the age limits for the country you are visiting. If you are getting work through an organisation you will be given this information.

Traditional organisations, such as Camp America, give you specific time off and even some time for a holiday at the end. More formal jobs, such as au-pair work, will specify the hours you have to work. For part-time work, such as an English Language assistant, you can have as much as two-thirds of the week free.

Temporary work means just that. It is likely to last only a few weeks or a few months, so you will constantly have to look for other jobs. If you are finding your own work, this is likely to make up the bulk of your work experience abroad.

If you are not sure what kind of work you want to do, read one or more of the publications listed at the back of this book, such as *Working Holidays*, to give you ideas. Jobs are as varied as your imagination. Why not try sheep farming, fruit picking, bar work or courier work, for example?

Apart from the organisations listed below, many newspapers and magazines contain small ads for jobs abroad. For au-pair work you can also look in *The Lady*.

WHEN AND HOW TO APPLY

It can take time to get the necessary papers and money together, so try to plan your work well in advance. A year is not too soon. This is especially important if the visa requirements are complicated.

There are certain regulations for obtaining work permits and visas for foreign countries. If you will be working in an EU country you do not need a work permit, but you will need a resident's permit if you are staying for more than three months. You can get one on arrival from the local town hall, police station or aliens' office. You will need to show proof that you have enough money to support yourself (e.g. money in a bank account). If you will be working for less than three months in the EU, then all you need is your passport. If you will be working between three months and a year in paid work experience or a temporary job, you will be issued with a residence permit for the period concerned. If your employer accepts that you are a student, you can work tax-free for six months in the EU.

Outside the EU you must make sure that you have the correct papers. Contact the relevant consulate or embassy well in advance. Also ensure that your employer registers your residency if this is required. Some countries have additional requirements – Australia, for example, requires you to have obtained your return ticket and to have about £1000 in savings before granting a work permit. You can register at employment agencies in member states of the EU and are entitled to the same help in finding jobs as that state's nationals.

Don't forget to ensure that your passport is up to date and will remain so for the duration of your year abroad. Some countries specify that it must be valid for longer than the period you expect to stay. If it will not be or is out of date, get it renewed at your nearest passport office (see Useful Addresses). If you need it quickly you can apply in person. You can get passport application or renewal forms at any post office. If you are working in the EU you will also need to get an E111 health form from your local post office (see chapter 2).

Warning

Although some students do work abroad illegally, it is not sensible. If you are found out you will be in serious trouble. Take time to sort out your papers well in advance so that you do not have to worry about the authorities.

Sex discrimination

Your gender should be no bar to any kind of job. Young men *can* now become au-pairs, for example. But in practice men are rarely placed as au-pairs because there is little or no call for them from families. Some agencies still take applications from girls only. If you want to work in a job that was traditionally done by the other sex, you may have to overcome outdated prejudices. This may mean providing proof of previous employment in a similar job.

Skills needed

You need to be adaptable, reliable, not easily upset if things go wrong, sociable, willing to work with other people and ready to make your own friends. Ideally you need to be outgoing, because you will have to go out and meet people for yourself.

For some jobs you will need particular skills such as a foreign language, a TEFL certificate, secretarial or driving skills, sports skills, etc. If you have not already got the ones you need, get them while you are planning your year out. If you are preparing a year in advance, you could use your holidays to acquire these skills.

Pay

You are unlikely to earn a lot working abroad. You will usually get the local pay for temporary workers or specified 'pocket money'. If going through an organisation you will be told what you can expect to be paid before you go. Allow for travel, board and lodging unless these are included as a part of your payment. You should also find out about the relevant tax laws for students in the country you will be working in to find out whether you are exempt or not.

Rights

In all countries you have the right to work free from sexual harassment or physical abuse – so report this to the authorities or organisation sending you if it occurs. Unfortunately standards in other countries are not always the same as ours, but there is no need to put up with anything you know to be wrong or unpleasant. If the worst happens, cut your losses and leave. It is better to be safe than sorry.

Where appropriate, you will have the right to board and lodging and you have the right to be paid what the employer has officially offered. In some jobs, such as au-pairing, you can expect a written contract or agreement. Try to get this for any job – but you are unlikely to get it for casual or temporary work. You also have the right to be officially declared a resident by your employer.

Safeguards

Apart from following common sense personal safety rules, do not accept a job abroad through an organisation unless you are satisfied with their answers to the following questions:

1 Do you arrange all documentation such as visas and work permits or do I do that?
2 If not, do you give advice on how to obtain the documentation?

3   Can I speak to people whom you've placed before?
4   How will you help me if things go wrong?
5   Is there a charge for registering with you?
6   What will I be paid? What is included – board and lodging, language lessons, paid holiday?
7   If I am being placed with a family, how do you vet them?
8   Do you vet employers?
9   Do you have representatives abroad?
10 What references must I supply, and when?
11 Will I get a written contract?
12 What will the work conditions be like?

Obviously, if you are finding your own work then many of these questions will not apply or will be unanswerable. However, you should bear them in mind as a basis for good work practices.

Problems of finding your own work

If applying for work directly, sort out documentation in good time and contact the relevant embassy as soon as possible. Try to arrange accommodation in advance. If possible get advice from someone who has already worked in the country you will be staying in, otherwise ask the tourist board for cheap lodgings when you get there. Or your employer may know of someone willing to rent you a room. Try the university for help from the student accommodation bureau. Again, make sure that your employer declares your residency, if applicable.

Au-pair agency applications

Applications through au-pair agencies will need to be accompanied by most or all of the following:

▶ application forms (possibly completed in the relevant language),

▶ passport photos,

▶ general photos of you (smiling!),

▶ two references,

▶ photocopy of your passport,

▶ a medical certificate dated less than three months previously, and its translation into the relevant language,

▶ photocopy of your birth certificate with your parents' first names, and its translation,

▶ photocopy of your latest exam certificates, and translation,

▶ a hand-written letter introducing yourself (preferably in the relevant language),

▶ two self-addressed envelopes, and

▶ international reply coupons from your post office.

The agency will specify which of these you require, but they are usually *all* needed at the time of application, so if you want to be an au-pair start collecting your documentation now!

Prospective US au-pairs are subject to strict regulations. You will have to show that you have at least 200 hours' experience with infants, 24 hours' training in child development and 8 hours' child safety training. You will also have to undergo psychometric testing to provide a personality profile.

£-££

Accueil Familial des Jeunes Etrangers

Accueil Familial places foreign girls in French families on an 'au-pair' basis. They are called family helps, according to French Ministry of Labour Regulations, and are subject to the Ministry's regulations. You will assist with the housework and look after children for about 30 hours a week. You may be asked to babysit two or three evenings a week. Officially there are no holidays during an au-pair stay, but you may come to an arrangement with the family.

HOW LONG IT WILL LAST
Six to eighteen months.

WHERE YOU CAN GO
You can be placed in Paris, its suburbs or different university cities or country towns. You cannot be guaranteed a place in a specific town because it depends on the needs of the families. However, if you do not get the town of your choice you will be offered an alternative.

PAYMENT
Full board and some pocket money, about 1650 francs per month. Meal times with the family are not included in working hours. One free day a week, usually Sunday. Social security (French social health insurance) is paid for by the family. For stays outside Paris, the family will refund the cost of the train ticket to and from their town of residence to Paris.

THE COST TO YOU
The cost is about 650 francs, including a non-refundable deposit of 220 francs. You have to find your own fares for travel to Paris and pay for the cost of compulsory French lessons for foreign students, without which you cannot be granted a Temporary Residence Permit.

WHO CAN APPLY
You must be unmarried, female, 18–27, and have a working knowledge of French to high school level. You must sign a contract with the family employing you for 6 months, and this can be extended to 18 months.

WHEN AND HOW TO APPLY
The best time to apply is early September. Contact the agency for an application form.

SELECTION PROCESS
The organisation will select a suitable placement and offer it to you.

PLACEMENT
You can decide whether to accept the placement offered.

TRAINING
You will be on trial for a week with the family and (unless in the 'Province') must then travel to Acceuil Familial's Paris office so that the organisers can explain the procedure for obtaining your Temporary Residence Permit and countersign your 'accord de placement', or contract, at the Foreign Labour Office. This is a binding contract and can only be broken for good reasons.

SUPPORT FOR PARTICIPANTS
The AFJE takes care of all the administrative details, registers you with insurance and gives information about courses in French. Once a month it organises cultural activities in Paris. It gives special attention to each girl and support if any problems arise, such as the need to change families.

£–£££   Au-pair USA

This offers gap year students the opportunity to spend a year working in America and living as part of an American family.

HOW LONG IT WILL LAST
One year.

WHERE YOU CAN GO
USA.

PAYMENT
You get payment of $139 (approximately £86) per week, two weeks' paid holiday, free return flights to the USA, free medical insurance, $500 to spend on college courses, and the opportunity for one month's travel in the USA at the end of the year. You are treated as an equal and provide a maximum of 45 hours of childcare per week in sole charge of the children.

THE COST TO YOU
None.

WHO CAN APPLY
You must be 18–26 years old and hold a valid driving licence, have practical childcare experience and be prepared to work abroad for a year.

WHEN AND HOW TO APPLY
Phone the New York headquarters for the name and address of the English office and then apply for a brochure and application form.

SELECTION PROCESS
Families and candidates are screened and interviewed.

PLACEMENT
Applicants are placed regionally in groups.

TRAINING
There is no specific training.

SUPPORT FOR PARTICIPANTS
Personal advice and guidance is given based on your initial inquiry. You are helped to choose a host family, organise visas and flights, etc. You are provided with a legal J-1 visa. In America colleagues are in contact throughout your stay and you are supported by a local coordinator. You are given the opportunity for regular contact and social activities with other au-pairs in your area.

££££ | AgriVenture

AgriVenture offers programmes for British citizens. Applicants are placed with a host family on a farm, to live and work with the family for the duration of the programme.

HOW LONG IT WILL LAST
The programmes last for periods of 5½ months to 14 months (two countries).

WHERE YOU WILL GO
Canada, USA, New Zealand, Australia or Japan.

PAYMENT
Applicants receive board and lodging and a wage, and holiday time is available during the programme and at completion. The AgriVenture motto is 'Don't Just Visit – LIVE it!'

THE COST TO YOU
All-inclusive costs start at £1790 and cover return tickets, full work/travel insurance, information day before departure, stopover (where applicable), three-day seminar on arrival in host country, all transfers to host family, administration (visas, placement, correspondence, supervision, etc), 24-hour emergency back-up worldwide and flight bag.

WHO CAN APPLY
Applicants must be aged 18–30, have had some experience of working in agriculture and need a full driving licence.

WHEN AND HOW TO APPLY
To receive a free brochure, telephone the AgriVenture freephone number.

SELECTION PROCESS
Short interview/chat locally to you with an AgriVenture representative.

PLACEMENT
AgriVenture places you on an enterprise as close to your first choice as possible, depending on your experience, etc.

TRAINING
There is an information day before you depart and you get a three-day seminar on arrival at your host country; ongoing training and new experiences with your family on a daily basis.

SUPPORT FOR PARTICIPANTS
There is 24-hour emergency back-up worldwide.

££ | The Athenian Nanny Agency

This agency places young women in work as nannies, au-pairs or mothers' helps. There are opportunities to take Greek language or dancing classes, visit islands or see ancient sites and museums.

HOW LONG IT WILL LAST
One year to 18 months on the Long Term or two to three months on the Summer Stay Programme.

WHERE YOU CAN GO
Greece.

PAYMENT
Payment is made monthly based on experience, number of children and nature of demands requested by the family. You also get all room and board expenses and a full in-depth arrival orientation.

THE COST TO YOU
There is no fee charged. You must find your outward fare to Greece.

WHO CAN APPLY
Suitable qualified or experiences females. Swimmers and non-smokers are preferred.

WHEN AND HOW TO APPLY
You can apply at any time. Send six IRCs with your photo, address, the length of stay and type of position required, with a short essay about your childcare experience and the reason you have chosen Greece.

SELECTION PROCESS
Applications are on a first come, first served basis.

PLACEMENT
This is based on the quality of your application and your experience and fluency of language skills. You do not need to know Greek.

TRAINING
None.

SUPPORT FOR PARTICIPANTS
You will have full support in the event of any problem

££ Avalon Au-Pairs

This is an au-pair agency and a distributor of brochures/application forms for USA au-pairing programmes.

HOW LONG IT WILL LAST
Be prepared to stay a minimum of six months.

WHERE YOU CAN GO
UK, Europe and USA.

PAYMENT
You get free accommodation and meals and pocket money of about £40 per week (which may be paid monthly). You will be given time to attend language courses and religious services if you wish. You will have one free day per week, including the evening.

THE COST TO YOU
Costs will include travel expenses and language course fees. You must have a return ticket to the UK or enough money to buy one at any time.

WHO CAN APPLY
You must be 18–27 (Germany age limit 24, Holland 25 years), single, with no dependants, and have at least a basic knowledge of the language of the country you will go to. Germany requires a good knowledge of the language; Finland and Holland do not require you to know the language. You should also have had some childcare experience.

WHEN AND HOW TO APPLY
Apply on an application form to the agency at any time, but at least two months before you wish to start. For the very few two- or three-month summer placements, the final date is 31 May.

SELECTION PROCESS
You must meet the criteria for the country you wish to au-pair in.

PLACEMENT
Your application is sent to approved agents who will fax the agency an offer. You then phone the family quickly and decide whether or not to accept the job. You should not travel to your family without a written offer from the agency.

TRAINING
None.

SUPPORT FOR PARTICIPANTS
You will have the support of the office of the foreign agency.

£££–££££ | BUNAC – Working Adventures Worldwide

BUNAC (British Universities North America Club) is a non-profit, non-political, student organisation with its own travel company. It is represented on British campuses by ex-participants. Programmes are organised by BUNAC to enable students and young people to live and work legally in other countries while earning enough money to travel and explore independently. Depending on the programme, you could work as a Summer Camp counsellor or kitchen and maintenance staff (KAMP) in America, or take part in a work/travel programme.

HOW LONG IT WILL LAST
Camp and KAMP work lasts from eight to ten weeks plus six weeks' travel time. Work/travel programmes can last from four to twelve months, depending on the destination.

WHERE YOU CAN GO
Gap year students can go to the USA, Canada, Australia, Ghana, South Africa, New Zealand and Jamaica. Programmes include Summer Camp USA, KAMP, and Work programmes in America, Canada, Australia, New Zealand, South Africa, Jamaica and Ghana.

PAYMENT
Summer Camp staff receive a minimum of between $540 and $600 on completion of their programme, depending on the type of camp you work in, free board and lodging, and travel to and from America and to and from New York to your camp. If you go on the Work programmes, your pay will depend on the type of jobs you get and how long you work. These programmes are potentially self-financing.

THE COST TO YOU
Camp registration fees are £63. The rest of the costs involved are 'loaned' to applicants and are then deemed to have been paid off once you have completed your work period. Visa requirements are that you must take at least $400 with you for travel after camp; you are advised to take twice as much. You also pay a visa processing fee, insurance and fee for a medical examination if required by your camp. For Work programmes you must be a member of BUNAC (cost £4). Other costs vary according to which programme option you choose, but you should expect to pay a registration fee/deposit of £84–£200, plus flights and insurance.

WHO CAN APPLY
All applicants must be 18 or over. Summer Camp USA and Work Australia/New Zealand also accept non-students. The age limits for Work Canada and Work New Zealand are 18–30, for Work Australia 18–25, for Jamaica and Africa 19–26 and for Summer Camp USA 19–35 (although qualified 18 year olds may also be accepted).

WHEN AND HOW TO APPLY
Apply to BUNAC for forms.

SELECTION PROCESS
Your application will be considered by the BUNAC Council.

PLACEMENT
You can either find a job before you go, find one once you are there or be sponsored by a national.

TRAINING
Before departure you attend orientations giving advice about jobs, accommodation and living and working in the relevant country.

SUPPORT FOR PARTICIPANTS
BUNAC helps with jobs, travel accommodation and emergencies. Back-up services are provided in each country.

££ | Camp America

Camp America places over 7500 young people each year in summer jobs on camps and with American families throughout the USA. There are a variety of opportunities. You could work as a camp counsellor, either as a specialist or general counsellor. Specialist counsellors teach different groups of children specific skills such as swimming or pottery. General counsellors are primarily responsible for the overall activity programme and supervisory care of a specific group of children. You could sign on for Campower, which includes administrative roles such as secretarial, plumbing, electrical, vehicle maintenance, horse/stable care, janitor, or laundry worker. Or you could be a Family Companion living with and working for an American host family, supervising the children and performing light household tasks. (See also Resort America p55).

HOW LONG IT WILL LAST
You must be available for at least nine weeks.

WHERE YOU CAN GO
USA.

PAYMENT
You get a free return flight to America, pocket money, visa sponsorship, orientations, free board and lodging in camp, and time for independent travel after camp. You will get a small amount of pocket money paid at the end of your placement. The amount will depend on your age and experience.

THE COST TO YOU
You pay a small deposit and insurance.

WHO CAN APPLY
You must be at least 18 years old and speak fluent English. There is no

upper age limit. You must like children and be calm, patient, flexible and (except for Campower) have experience supervising children. You will have a good chance of being placed if you have a specialist skill which is useful on camp.

WHEN AND HOW TO APPLY
Write to Camp America for a brochure and complete an application form.

SELECTION PROCESS
You attend a local interview.

PLACEMENT
By Camp America.

TRAINING
Unless you go straight to camp, you get orientation and accommodation beforehand in New York.

SUPPORT FOR PARTICIPANTS
At the end of your stay you get a signed completion certificate and your future employers can ask Camp America for a reference. Camp America provides 24-hour emergency assistance for staff throughout your stay.

££-£££££

Challenge Educational Services

This company organises a variety of programmes for gap year students. Challenge Educational also specialises in voluntary work experience in the USA for undergraduates and graduates, and offers an Academic High School programme and numerous language learning options in France. *Work Experience in the USA* gives you the chance to work in an American business or industry and to experience the American style of doing business. Challenge Educational also provides French language courses in France.

HOW LONG IT WILL LAST
Voluntary work placements – internships – last from 8 to 12 weeks and French language programmes from one week to a full academic year.

WHERE YOU CAN GO
San Francisco in the USA or France.

PAYMENT
None.

THE COST TO YOU
Work experience fees are around £775 to £2640, including interview and application, plus the cost of accommodation. The price depends on the length of stay and the type of accommodation. Language courses cost from about £400 to £3940. Flights and spending money are not included in the language programmes or internships.

WHO CAN APPLY
Work experience applicants must be 18–25 and can be gap year students, undergraduates or have work experience in a related field. To spend an academic year in a High School you must be aged 15 to 18.

WHEN AND HOW TO APPLY
Apply to Challenge Educational for brochures and application forms. Apply from four to six months before departure.

SELECTION PROCESS
By interview.

PLACEMENT
You choose whether to accept a family or placement offered. If you apply for work experience every effort will be made to find you a placement in your preferred field, but you will also be asked to give an alternative field of placement.

TRAINING
On-the-job for internships.

SUPPORT FOR PARTICIPANTS
Work experience students are supported by an Internship Coordinator. Students at High School will be supported by a local Community Counsellor.

£-£££

Childcare International Ltd

Childcare International is a specialist recruitment agency that can arrange au-pair placements for gap year students in the USA or Europe.

HOW LONG IT WILL LAST
In America the placements are for one-year visa-supported stays only. European placements are for two or three months in the summer and six months or more at other times of the year.

WHERE YOU CAN GO
USA, Europe.

PAYMENT
In the USA you will get at least $139.50 per week; au-pairs in Europe can expect about £40 per week and mothers' helps about £75+. You will get a bedroom and meals, time off and some holiday. For USA placements only, you get a free round-trip flight from London to your host family's home and $500 towards university level education courses.

THE COST TO YOU
For the USA programme you must put down a $500 training deposit which is refunded in full when you successfully complete the programme. For a European placement you pay a fee of £40 plus VAT on confirmation of a host family and will have to pay your own fares

to the country concerned. You must also pay for your language tuition.

WHO CAN APPLY

For the USA you must be between 18 and 26. You must be able to supply written childcare references, such as babysitting. If you wish to work with children younger than two years of age you must provide written references showing that you have a minimum of 200 hours' experience for under-twos. European au-pairs/mothers' helps must be between 18 and 27, male or female, and single.

WHEN AND HOW TO APPLY

Apply at least two months before you want to start. Ask Childcare International for an application form. Placements are available all year.

SELECTION PROCESS

Selection is by application and interview.

PLACEMENT

Placements are made on the basis of your application and an interview.

TRAINING

Applicants for the USA receive a Childcare International training course before placement.

SUPPORT FOR PARTICIPANTS

You will receive ongoing support from Childcare International's representative agencies abroad.

££

CIEE – Council on International Educational Exchange

The CIEE arranges international work placements, which are organised through its International Work Programme. There are opportunities for full-time students or recent graduates. Some programmes only take graduates and others only full-time students. One scheme of particular interest to gap year students is Internship Canada, which gives you the chance to experience the Canadian work environment. It will help you improve your French if you do your internship in French-speaking areas. The CIEE also offers work/travel programmes in the USA and Australia, as well as many study opportunities (see chapter 10).

HOW LONG IT WILL LAST

For Internship Canada you can stay up to twelve months, starting at any time during the year.

WHERE YOU CAN GO

Canada.

PAYMENT
It will depend on the type of job you get.

THE COST TO YOU
Programme fees are about £150 for Canada. You will need to find your fares and living expenses.

WHO CAN APPLY
For Internship Canada you must be a gap year student with an unconditional offer from a UK university or college, or a full-time higher education student.

WHEN AND HOW TO APPLY
Contact CIEE for further information and an application form.

SELECTION PROCESS
Your application will be considered by CIEE.

PLACEMENT
You are responsible for finding your own work in Canada, but the CIEE will give you information to help you.

TRAINING
All programmes provide pre-departure advice and information.

SUPPORT FOR PARTICIPANTS
The CIEE provides in-country support throughout your stay.

££-££££ | EIL

EIL arranges many different kinds of programmes that enable people to travel abroad and learn about and understand another culture. Programmes include language courses in Europe, South America and Japan, university and college placements in the USA, or sports-related placements in the USA. Of particular interest to gap year students are its European Voluntary Service and Au-pair or Homestay programmes. Homestay gives you the opportunity to live with a selected family in the country of your choice. (See chapter 6.)

££ | Eurocamp

Eurocamp can arrange courier work on campsites. You could work as a campsite courier, children's courier, area administrator or a montage/demontage assistant (someone who sets up and dismantles the tents). Those over 21 can work as site supervisors.

WHERE YOU CAN GO
France, Italy, Belgium, Germany, Luxembourg, Holland, Austria, Switzerland, Spain, Corsica, Sardinia, Denmark.

PAYMENT
The average pay is about £95 per week, paid directly into your bank account.

THE COST TO YOU
You will need to pay for your meals (except for montage/demontage assistants).

WHO CAN APPLY
You must be 18+ (21+ for site supervisors) and preferably have a good working knowledge of a major European language. Previous customer experience is preferred.

WHEN AND HOW TO APPLY
Apply to Eurocamp Overseas Recruitment Department.

SELECTION PROCESS
The skills you can offer will be taken into account.

PLACEMENT
Eurocamp will allocate you to an area where they think you will be suited and where they think customers will benefit from your skills. You can state a preferred area and this will be given consideration; however, there is no guarantee you will be placed in that region.

TRAINING
You receive intensive training in all aspects of campsite life.

SUPPORT FOR PARTICIPANTS
Once on-site, you receive ongoing support and assistance from the Eurocamp Overseas team, who will also provide feedback on your performance.

££ | French Encounters

This is a small, independent enterprise based in two châteaux in Normandy that runs study field-trips for 10–13 year olds. It takes approximately eight young people with A-level French who are taking a year out to act as 'animateurs/animatrices'. You would accompany coaches and give commentaries on places to be visited; supervise children on visits and picnics; organise indoor and outdoor activities; encourage children to speak French and eat French food, and generally make their stay rewarding and pleasant. You would work approximately 35 hours per week but be on call 24 hours a day.

HOW LONG IT WILL LAST
The job lasts from mid-February for up to four months.

WHERE YOU CAN GO
Normandy, France.

PAYMENT
Full board and lodging and generous pocket money. All transport costs and insurance are provided.

WHO CAN APPLY
You should be 18–22, enthusiastic, have good organisational skills, be good at working in a team, self-disciplined and have a sense of humour. It is essential to have experience of working with children and A-level French with good oral skills.

WHEN AND HOW TO APPLY
Apply before the end of August.

SELECTION PROCESS
Interviews are usually held in the first week in October.

TRAINING
You will attend a compulsory training course and debriefing before and after your period of work.

SUPPORT FOR PARTICIPANTS
The Bromsgrove office of French Encounters is always happy to supply further details.

£ Home From Home

This is an au-pair agency.

HOW LONG IT WILL LAST
There are more vacancies from September to June but you can also apply for a short summer stay from June to September.

WHERE YOU CAN GO
Europe, particularly France, Spain, Italy, Holland, Belgium and Germany. You will do about 30 hours' work a week, including childcare, light housework, ironing and meal preparation.

PAYMENT
You will receive a minimum of £30 pocket money and at least one day off per week, and time to attend college and study.

THE COST TO YOU
£40 placement fee and travel costs.

WHO CAN APPLY
Young men and women aged 18–27 (Belgium and Italy will take you at 17).

WHEN AND HOW TO APPLY
Complete an application form and return it with the relevant documents. Your dossier will be sent to an agent abroad who will match you with a suitable family.

SELECTION PROCESS
Your acceptance will be based on your application form and references.

PLACEMENT
The foreign agent will send details of a family which will be passed to you. You talk to the family before making your decision.

TRAINING
There is no specific training given.

SUPPORT FOR PARTICIPANTS
Provided by the agents in the country you work in.

££ | Inter-Séjours

An agency placing young women or men in au-pair or 'live in' work. On the Au-pair Plus scheme you will work two or three afternoons a week looking after children, and be paid. On Demi Pair you will work about three hours per day with two evenings babysitting, for board and lodging only. In Canada the scheme is as a 'live-in caregiver' and you are considered to be a temporary worker and will need to get a work permit before you arrive. You are normally expected to attend language lessons locally.

HOW LONG IT WILL LAST
The usual stay is from six to 18 months, but some stays of two or three months are possible during the summer vacation.

WHERE YOU CAN GO
For au-pair work you can go to France, Spain, Italy, Ireland, Germany, Austria, Canada, Australia – or Britain.

PAYMENT
On Demi Pair you either get nothing or perhaps a little pocket money. For other au-pair or live-in work, the amount of pocket money varies according to the country and is determined by the family concerned. But generally the amount is designed to cover weekly trips out, transport, telephone calls, stamps, etc.

THE COST TO YOU
You pay 850 French francs. You will normally pay your own travel expenses, although some families contribute if you are spending a year as a student. Inter-Séjours can arrange tickets at preferential prices. Language lessons will cost extra.

WHO CAN APPLY
You must be 18–28 and unmarried without children. The minimum age is 17 in Spain and Ireland and 18 elsewhere. For Canada you must be 20+. Normally you need some knowledge of the language of the country to which you are applying.

WHEN AND HOW TO APPLY
Complete an Inter-Séjours application form and provide the relevant documentation.

SELECTION PROCESS
Your application form will be considered.

PLACEMENT
On receipt of your application form the organisation will try to find a suitable family for you. You will receive a letter as soon as possible giving details of the family. You are encouraged to make initial contact with the family before departure.

TRAINING
There is no specific training.

SUPPORT FOR PARTICIPANTS
You will have the services of a local representative to help you if difficulties arise. If you are staying for more than three months, you have the right to change families if necessary. You also get help and advice from Inter-Séjours.

£–££ | PGL Adventure

PGL provide activity courses for children and can offer young people seasonal work. They recruit about 2000 staff to work at their centres in Britain, France and Spain. Job opportunities include group leaders, activity instructors, catering staff, administrators, support staff, couriers and other vacancies.

HOW LONG IT WILL LAST
The work is seasonal from February to November.

WHERE YOU CAN GO
Britain, France and Spain.

PAYMENT
In the UK new staff under 26 receive an allowance of £50–£60 per week. In subsequent years you are paid a wage and get about £70 in hand after expenses. In France and Spain you will get £50 per week in local currency. Suitably qualified people in specialist roles receive higher rates. The cost of all instruction, assessment equipment and accommodation costs for those taking National Governing Body activity awards is paid for by PGL. Whatever work you do, you will receive accommodation and all meals.

THE COST TO YOU
None unless you are taking sports awards, in which case all you pay are the membership log book and registration fees charged by the membership body.

WHO CAN APPLY
You must normally be 18+ although for some jobs, such as driver, you must be 21. For Adventure Europe centre activities, preference is given to applicants over 20. Applicants for administrator jobs in France and Spain must

be able to speak the language fluently, and couriers need to have a sound grasp of the language. For specialist jobs, specific relevant qualifications may be required and applicants therefore tend to be slightly older.

WHEN AND HOW TO APPLY

Complete a PGL application form and apply as early as possible. You will need to supply two references. Ideally you should be available from February although vacancies arise throughout the season, which ends in November. The main staff intake is February to May.

SELECTION PROCESS

If the application form seems satisfactory you will be shortlisted and your referees contacted. This does not mean that you will automatically be offered a job. When your referees have been contacted you may be offered work. If you have any relevant activity or vocational qualifications, you must enclose photocopies of these with your application or they will not be considered.

PLACEMENT

You can request a particular centre but you can only be placed at a centre which has a vacancy. The more you limit your choice, the less likely you are to be placed. Stating your job preference does not stop PGL considering you for other jobs, as they need to place people in jobs to which they think they are well suited and for which they have vacancies.

TRAINING

PGL runs a vocational training programme as a three-stage apprenticeship scheme. New staff receive a comprehensive induction and training package related to the job. If you work for PGL in subsequent years you can take appropriate NVQs at levels 2–4.

SUPPORT FOR PARTICIPANTS

Training and support throughout the work period is provided by PGL.

££ Pro Filia

This is for students wishing to improve their French and willing to work as an au-pair. There is a separate Pro Filia branch in Lausanne.

HOW LONG IT WILL LAST

You must be prepared to work from August to September for at least one year.

WHERE YOU CAN GO

Geneva, Switzerland.

PAYMENT

You receive pocket money of about 710 Swiss francs per month, full board, accident insurance, opportunity to attend a language school and one day off a week and 4–5 weeks' holiday during a twelve-month stay. During the holidays you receive pay of about SF27 per day to compensate for food and lodging as well as your pocket money.

THE COST TO YOU

The registration fee is 30 Swiss francs. Swiss social and state tax (about SF115 per month), health insurance, fee for language studies (which are compulsory for a minimum of four hours per week – about SF1000) and bus fares of about SF35 per month. You must also pay for your return fare to Switzerland.

WHO CAN APPLY

You must be between 18 and 30, a non-smoker and have a basic knowledge of French.

WHEN AND HOW TO APPLY

Obtaining a work permit takes at least two months, so apply in plenty of time and ensure you have a valid passport. Apply from February but definitely by June. The application form must be completed in French and be accompanied by a CV in French, some 'nice' photos, two or three references and a recent medical certificate.

SELECTION PROCESS

Selection is based on your application documents.

PLACEMENT

An interested family will contact you by phone or letter. You can accept them or choose another family.

TRAINING

There is no specific training.

SUPPORT FOR PARTICIPANTS

Assistance with legal requirements, advice and guidance, and help if any problems arise.

££ Resort America

This is run by Camp America and provides summer resort work and travel in the USA.

HOW LONG IT WILL LAST

The placements last from 10 to 16 weeks, with time for independent travel afterwards.

WHERE YOU CAN GO

Resorts are situated across the entire USA.

PAYMENT

You receive free flights, help in getting your visa, orientations, food, accommodation and support while in the USA. You will be paid a small amount of pocket money at the end of the placement. The sum will depend on your age, qualifications and experience.

THE COST TO YOU
You pay a small deposit and insurance.

WHO CAN APPLY
You must be over 19 and a student to apply. There is no upper age limit.

WHEN AND HOW TO APPLY
Contact Resort America for an application form and brochure.

SELECTION PROCESS
This is by local interview.

PLACEMENT
By Resort America.

TRAINING
You get orientation beforehand.

SUPPORT FOR PARTICIPANTS
You get support from Resort America while you are in the USA.

££-£££

Verein für Internationale Jungendarbeit

This is a German Protestant women's organisation affiliated to the World YWCA. It places au-pairs in Germany – both men and women. You will help with the children and housework and if both parents are working will have sole care for a few hours during the day. You will be expected to work about 30 hours a week and babysit two or three evenings a week. You will get one day off a week. You are not entitled to holidays but it is customary to give paid holidays after a stay of six months. In your free time you can attend language classes and take part in cultural activities and have the chance to go to church if you wish.

HOW LONG IT WILL LAST
You should be prepared to stay at least six months, but families prefer people who can stay for one year or the academic year.

WHERE YOU CAN GO
Germany.

PAYMENT
You will get a room of your own, full board and pocket money of about DM400 per month and a ticket for public transport to the language school and the au-pair club.

THE COST TO YOU
There is no agency fee, but you will have to pay your fares to and from Germany and the costs of your language school tuition.

WHO CAN APPLY
You must be between 18 and 24, a non-smoker, single and without dependents. You must have had some childcare and household experience and be able to communicate reasonably in German.

WHEN AND HOW TO APPLY
Apply for application forms and return them completed with the specified documents.

SELECTION PROCESS
Selection is based on your application form.

PLACEMENT
Contact the head office of Verein für Internationale Jungendarbeit which can arrange au-pair jobs in all areas of Germany.

TRAINING
None.

SUPPORT FOR PARTICIPANTS
You can keep in touch with your local Verein für Internationale Jungendarbeit office which will be pleased to help you with information and advice. Many of the offices have an au-pair club attached.

£££-££££   Visitoz

Visitoz can place you in working holidays in a wide variety of outback jobs, in the hospitality industry, or rural tourism industries. It can guarantee travel placements to fit in with your holiday plans. Visitoz can help with further work placements, act as a contact point and be a source of support while you are in Australia. Many of the jobs are on outback properties and may include working with horses, tractor driving and maintenance. Visitoz will collect you from Brisbane airport and take you to stay at a training farm to learn the necessary skills. It will help you arrange an Australian bank account, medical card, tax file number and student ID. You then choose from a list of current vacancies and travel to your first job.

HOW LONG IT WILL LAST
Placements can be arranged to fit in with your holiday plans.

WHERE YOU CAN GO
Australia.

PAYMENT
Typical wages start at $250 per week for all types of work, board and lodging provided. Good workers quickly get better rates.

THE COST TO YOU
The fee to join the Visitoz scheme is £385, including a non-refundable application fee of £10. You will need to pay return fares to Australia.

WHO CAN APPLY
You can be a pre-university, undergraduate or postgraduate student.

WHEN AND HOW TO APPLY
Contact Visitoz for an application form.

SELECTION PROCESS
According to your application form.

PLACEMENT
After your stay on the training farm you choose work from a suitable list of vacancies.

TRAINING
Visitoz provides basic training in the agricultural and other skills need for arrival in Australia. You will learn the basic skills for work on the training farm when you first arrive.

SUPPORT FOR PARTICIPANTS
Dan and Joanna Burnedt, who run the Springfield training farm, are available at any time during your stay in Australia to arrange further work or travel breaks and to give help with any problems, including illness or injury.

£-£££

Young Farmers' Clubs – International Farm Experience Programme

This is suitable for people who have had experience of farming and provides work experience in agriculture and horticulture. For some placements a knowledge of agriculture is not necessary.

HOW LONG IT WILL LAST
Placements last from three to twelve months, usually beginning at a time of your choice.

WHERE YOU CAN GO
Austria, Australia, Belgium, Bulgaria, Canada, China, Czech Republic, Denmark, Finland, France, Germany, Greece, Holland, Hungary, Italy, Norway, Spain, Sweden, Switzerland, Poland, New Zealand or USA.

PAYMENT
You will be paid for the work you do and can expect to cover your costs.

THE COST TO YOU
Between about £250 and £1000 for fares (depending on where you go) plus insurance and a registration fee.

WHO CAN APPLY
You must be between 18 and 28 and have at least two years' experience in the industry (one of which can be at college).

WHEN AND HOW TO APPLY
Apply to the YFC.

SELECTION PROCESS
This is based on your application.

PLACEMENT
You cannot be guaranteed a place and you may be asked to accept another country or defer for a year.

TRAINING
You may be able to take four-week language courses before EC placements.

SUPPORT FOR PARTICIPANTS
From the YFC.

voluntary and community work in the UK

VOLUNTARY AND COMMUNITY WORK IN THE UK

If you are looking for a useful and rewarding way of spending your year off and do not need to earn money, then consider voluntary or community work. These kinds of jobs involve helping people either in general or to help them realise a particular project, such as environmental improvement. Jobs can range from helping the mentally or physically disabled, teaching children skills, improving the environment, clearing canals, painting and decorating for a voluntary group and many more.

The difference between voluntary and community work is a fine one. *Voluntary* means that you should not expect to be paid for your work, although sometimes you might get board, lodging or a little pocket money. Often you have to pay a small amount for your board. *Community* means that it is a project or organisation that is doing something for its local community. Again the work is unpaid but worthwhile. The two terms often coincide in one project.

Usually it is enough to be willing to work hard and become involved in whatever project you want to join. Be prepared to work for the full time you have agreed. Commitment is a vital part of these projects and schemes can fall apart if volunteers leave earlier than agreed without good reason.

Some projects or organisations require particular skills. If you want to work with children, for example, you may need to show that you have had previous experience. You may need to be able to drive and hold a valid full driving licence. You might need word-processing or computer skills. It all depends on what kind of voluntary work you want to do. However, if you do not have the right skills for one job, then there are so many others available that you should have no trouble finding work for your year out. Obviously, if you have a particular skill to offer, such as carpentry skills, first aid qualifications or previous experience in similar work, then this will make finding voluntary work easier.

There is almost unlimited scope for voluntary and/or community work. If none of the organisations listed here interests you, try asking your local library or council if they have a list of local projects or voluntary schemes. Sometimes large charitable organisations do take one or two gap year students, but many do not or prefer older people or graduates. However, if you particularly want to work for one of these, try contacting them directly.

Religion

Many voluntary and community projects are run by religious groups. Some require volunteers to be committed members of that religion. Others will accept anyone who is committed to the aims of the project. I have indicated any particular religious requirements for relevant schemes. If you are interested in one of them, make sure that you agree with the aims and ideas of the organisation. Your parents, teacher or religious leader will be able to advise whether the scheme is appropriate for you.

£ Camphill Communities

The Camphill movement was founded by Dr Karl König, a psychiatrist and educator who pioneered education for children with special needs. The first Camphill Special Schools were opened in 1940. Camphill Communities now consists of centres for adults with special needs, special schools, and further education and training centres. The work in the communities is based on the teachings of Rudolph Steiner. There are now over 90 centres in 20 countries. Most of the centres welcome gap year volunteers, who work alongside both residents and other co-workers to support adults and children in the communities.

Permanent staff, volunteers and students – all called co-workers – live in individual houses and all take part in the day-to-day running of the house communities and the land and grounds. Your major responsibility would be to help the group of three to four residents in your care over matters of personal hygiene, care of possessions, interests, recreational activities and participation in the daily routine. Everyone works a six-day week with one day off. There is no shift system. Any of the communities can provide you with a list of all Camphill Communities. For some of the addresses see under Camphill in the address list.

HOW LONG IT WILL LAST
All volunteers are asked to stay for a minimum of one year, although shorter stays are sometimes considered, for example from Christmas until early July.

WHERE YOU CAN GO
There are now 90 communities in 20 countries including England – Austria, Botswana, Canada, Estonia, Finland, France, Germany, The Netherlands, Ireland, Northern Ireland, Norway, Poland, Russia, Scotland, South Africa, Sweden, Switzerland, USA and Wales.

PAYMENT
You get free board and lodging and about £29 per week pocket money.

THE COST TO YOU
None, but you will have to pay your travel expenses.

WHO CAN APPLY
Camphill prefer students to be nearer the age of 20 when working in the centres for adults with special needs, but take people from 18 upwards to work in the schools and further education and training centres.

WHEN AND HOW TO APPLY
Contact individual communities for details of how to apply.

SELECTION PROCESS
Selection is at the discretion of individual communities.

TRAINING
You will be helped by a more experienced co-worker to learn to help, encourage and educate your group. The Camphill Foundation Year Certificate is open to all co-workers who have committed themselves to one year in Camphill. It consists of house tutorials, a weekly foundation course, weekly artistic activities, monthly tutorials and possibly workshops in the holidays.

SUPPORT FOR PARTICIPANTS
You can turn to your housemother or more experienced co-workers. You can also share concerns and experiences at a weekly house meeting.

SOME CAMPHILL COMMUNITIES IN THE UK:
Camphill Rudolph Steiner School Aberdeen: this is a residential school for children in need of special care. You must be 19 years or over and able to converse easily in English. It offers voluntary work for one school year and you will be eligible to take the Camphill Foundation Year course. Write to the School for an application form. Volunteers are taken each term, i.e. Michaelmas, Christmas, Easter and Summer.

Camphill Community Beannachar: Beannachar is a community providing work, training and education for young adults with special needs in the 17 to 30 age range. The daily work involves both the volunteers (co-workers) and students according to their abilities and includes organic biodynamic gardening, herb work, farming, cooking, cleaning, candle-making, laundry and weaving. Everyone is expected to join in the cultural life. Most volunteers are gap students and mostly from other European countries. You must be over 19 and speak fluent English. Beannachar offers the one-year Foundation course and a tutor system of support.

Mourne Grange Camphill Village Community: this is a village community for adults with special needs. Volunteers live and work for a year alongside those who need help, together with permanent voluntary workers and their families. Volunteers live in one of twelve house communities and take a full part in all aspects of home life. Work might be in a workshop – pottery, woodwork, weaving, bakery, laundry – or in a house or garden or farm. You must be willing to share community life with mentally handicapped adults and be at least 19.

Pennine Camphill Community: this is a College of Education and Training for young people with special needs. The work involves becoming involved with the daily running of the house and with three or four students whom you will encourage with friendly advice on personal hygiene, care of possessions, etc. The Community welcomes gap year students if they can commit for twelve months and will spend the time at Pennine, excluding holidays.

£ Careforce

The aim of Careforce is to serve evangelical churches and organisations by placing Christian volunteers where their help is most needed in the UK and Ireland. It enables Christians from the UK and other countries to serve as volunteers in an area of need alongside local Christians.

HOW LONG IT WILL LAST
One year.

WHERE YOU CAN GO
UK or Ireland.

PAYMENT
Weekly pocket money and full board and lodging.

THE COST TO YOU
Everyone is asked to raise some financial support to help cover Careforce central costs, but this is entirely voluntary and is not a condition of acceptance.

WHO CAN APPLY
You must be Christian and aged 18 to 25.

WHEN AND HOW TO APPLY
Contact Careforce for an application form. You will need to complete this and supply three references.

SELECTION PROCESS
After your application form and references have been received, you attend a personal interview with Careforce leading to a final visit to a possible placement before acceptance.

PLACEMENT
You will be placed where there is need and will join local churches where resources are scarce as well as join in residential programmes and other projects.

TRAINING

Careforce provides two training courses for all its volunteers during their year. However, the essence of the training is hands-on training on placement alongside trained and qualified colleagues. Experiential learning is the main training mode.

SUPPORT FOR PARTICIPANTS

Full support, both work and pastoral, is given to all Careforce volunteers within their placements. This is given by local Careforce volunteers, a dedicated Careforce staff worker who will visit each volunteer at least twice on their placement, and from the volunteer's home church, family and friends who are asked to stay involved throughout the year.

££££

Church Mission Society (CMS)

This society has been involved in world mission for nearly 200 years. It runs a Make A Difference (UK) programme which gives young Christians the opportunity to experience another culture for six to eighteen months through church-run projects. They also run a Make A Difference (Overseas) programme for those aged 21–50. CMS also has an Encounter programme which arranges travel as a group to visit the Christian community of another culture and share in their lives.

HOW LONG IT WILL LAST

Make a Difference programmes last between six and eighteen months. Encounter lasts from three to five weeks.

WHERE YOU CAN GO

With Make A Difference (UK) you work in the inner cities, rural areas, suburbia – anywhere with a culture different from your own group in the UK. With Make A Difference (Overseas) placements are in many countries in Africa, Asia, the Middle East or Eastern Europe. Encounter locations vary.

PAYMENT

None, but CMS pays for training and reorientation costs and the cost of pre-placement travel.

THE COST TO YOU

You will have to budget for living expenses, and a UK placement will cost approximately £1000, depending on its location and length of stay. An overseas placement costs approximately £2500 and an Encounter visit £700–£900.

WHO CAN APPLY

You need to be aged 18–30 and a committed Christian currently involved in your local church or Christian Union.

WHEN AND HOW TO APPLY
For a UK placement apply by the end of May for summer departure or end of October for a winter departure. For an Encounter visit apply by 18 April. Contact CMS for a form.

SELECTION PROCESS
The application procedure involves a two-stage interviewing procedure; references and medical clearance are also required.

PLACEMENT
During the Selection process applicants will be asked about their desired location and work placement. However, placement will depend on the needs of the community.

TRAINING
For the Make A Difference programmes there is a training period of 10 days which all participants must attend and involves considering the issues of cross-cultural mission and preparation to adapt to living in a new culture or social situation. For the Encounter programme there are two weekends of training so that participants can gain the maximum from the experience. CMS feels that appropriate training is essential to ensure that the experience is beneficial for both the participants and the host projects.

SUPPORT FOR PARTICIPANTS
CMS considers it important in a short-term placement that people receive an appropriate level of support from their host and from CMS. CMS is committed to giving that support and will do everything it can to ensure that the placement is a positive experience.

£-££

Conservation Volunteers Northern Ireland (CVNI)

This is part of British Trust for Conservation Volunteers and provides opportunities for involvement in environmental conservation work such as drystone walling, tree planting, path creation, river clearance, etc. You could work as a Volunteer Officer (VO), with responsibilities varying from setting up and organising projects for volunteer groups to leading residentials and maintaining tools and vehicles. If you would like to spend an extended time with CVNI but do not want the extra responsibilities of being a VO, all the CVNI offices offer long-term volunteering opportunities as Long Term Volunteers (LTVs). Other volunteering opportunities include regular weekend or weekday opportunities. There are also short working holidays available at a small cost.

HOW LONG IT WILL LAST
All VOs are accepted on a one-month trial basis initially, and you are normally asked to commit yourself to at least six months.

WHERE YOU CAN GO
Northern Ireland.

PAYMENT
All VOs receive an annual, free Natural Break holiday and BTCV merchandising to the value of £10. In some cases you may get free accommodation. Residential facilities for VOs exist at CVNI centres in Belfast, Fermanagh and Newry. All VOs are provided with suitable protective clothing.

THE COST TO YOU
Usually accommodation, food, travel, etc.

WHO CAN APPLY
For general volunteering you need to be 16 years or over, have good spoken English, a reasonable level of education, enthusiasm and adaptability. VOs are usually older because many posts require a driving licence and, in some cases where driving a minibus is required, you must have held a licence for a year and be over 21. Ideally you should have knowledge of practical environmental work and experience of working with volunteers.

WHEN AND HOW TO APPLY
Write directly to the Belfast (Volunteer) Information Officer requesting an application form and vacancy list. You can express an interest in vacancies on the list.

SELECTION PROCESS
If you are being considered for a post you will be invited to attend an informal interview and to stay for a day or two.

PLACEMENT
When a vacancy arises, all those who have expressed an interest are considered.

TRAINING
You will receive a job description and full training.

All VOs have a training profile drawn up for them and in some cases this may include externally-run training courses. All VOs have free access to CVNI's training programme, and are encouraged to qualify for National Vocational Qualifications.

SUPPORT FOR PARTICIPANTS
Volunteers work as part of a team.

£-££

Corrymeela Community

The Corrymeela Community is a community whose members come from all Christian traditions. It aims to further the healing of social, religious and political divisions, and provides a number of programmes for schools, youth, families, Christian Education and open events as well as volunteer opportunities at its Ballycastle centre. Twelve volunteers are chosen each year to help with the running of the centre. You would be responsible for working with groups of all kinds who use the centre, visiting them prior to their stay and maintaining a link with the group. You would also be involved in practical tasks such as catering, laundry, reception, etc.

HOW LONG IT WILL LAST
Twelve one-year and two six-month volunteers are chosen annually.

WHERE YOU CAN GO
Ballycastle, County Antrim.

PAYMENT
You get food and accommodation and a small living allowance. You will get eight days off per month and four weeks' holiday in the year.

THE COST TO YOU
Travel and incidental expenses.

WHO CAN APPLY
You must usually be between 18 and 30.

WHEN AND HOW TO APPLY
Year-long volunteers must apply before 1 March to start in September. Six-month volunteers start in March and should apply during the previous September.

SELECTION PROCESS
A shortlist of year applicants will be made in March, who will be asked to attend an interview in March or April. A similar process for six-month volunteers takes place in October. Corrymeela prefer candidates to visit the centre to meet staff and hear first-hand about the life and work.

TRAINING
You learn on-the-job.

SUPPORT FOR PARTICIPANTS
Volunteers live in a Community house with other members of staff.

CSV (Community Service Volunteers)

CSV is a UK charity that involves 3000 people every year in voluntary work. CSV guarantees to find you a placement working directly with people who need your help. You normally start work within a month of interview.

HOW LONG IT WILL LAST
You must be able to commit for a minimum of four months, up to a maximum of twelve months.

WHERE YOU CAN GO
Anywhere in the UK.

PAYMENT
Free accommodation, food or food allowance, £24.50 per week living allowance and out-of-pocket expenses.

THE COST TO YOU
Nothing.

WHO CAN APPLY
You must be between 16 and 35 and be prepared to work full-time away from home. You do not need specific qualifications.

WHEN AND HOW TO APPLY
Apply at any time throughout the year. Application forms are available from CSV.

SELECTION PROCESS
Selection is at the discretion of CSV.

PLACEMENT
A placement is guaranteed to everyone who wants one.

TRAINING
You will receive regular supervision at your project.

SUPPORT FOR PARTICIPANTS
Back-up support is provided by your local CSV office.

£ | Edinburgh Cyrenians

This provides services to homeless young people in Edinburgh and the Lothian Region. There are two Communities in Edinburgh and West Lothian, which consist of people aged 18–30 who have been referred to the Cyrenians by social workers. Volunteers work alongside residents and other volunteers sharing household tasks, leisure activities and contributing to Community meetings. You will be given particular responsibilities with other volunteers.

HOW LONG IT WILL LAST
You must be prepared to commit yourself for six months.

WHERE YOU CAN GO
Edinburgh or West Lothian, Scotland.

PAYMENT
You get £29 per week pocket money, full board and lodging and a time-off flat. Holiday and leaving grants are available.

THE COST TO YOU
Travel to the Community and incidental expenses.

WHO CAN APPLY
You must be 18–30, open-minded and willing to learn. You will need a strong sense of responsibility and commitment as well as energy, enthusiasm and a sense of humour.

WHEN AND HOW TO APPLY
Write to the Edinburgh Cyrenians for an application form.

SELECTION PROCESS
Decisions will be made based on the detailed information required on the application form.

PLACEMENT
This will be in one of the two Communities.

TRAINING
You will be given full training.

SUPPORT FOR PARTICIPANTS
You will receive regular supervision from the non-residential social worker managing your Community.

£-££

Ffestiniog Railway

The Ffestiniog Railway was opened in 1836 to carry slates from mines in Blaenau Ffestiniog to Portmadog harbour. It was closed in 1946 and The Ffestiniog Railway Society was set up in 1954 to help rebuild it. It was finally restored in 1982, but there is still the need for an all-year-round volunteer force to work with the permanent staff. The work is arranged by departments: Operating – operating the trains and stations; Workshops – building and maintaining locomotives and carriages; Civil Engineering – tracks and structures; Buildings, Parks, Gardens & Electrical – looking after the railway buildings and environment; Sales & Catering; Signals & Telecommunications.

HOW LONG IT WILL LAST
Volunteers are needed all year round.

WHERE YOU CAN GO
Vale of Ffestiniog, Wales.

PAYMENT
None.

THE COST TO YOU
You will need to budget for accommodation. Look on the Ffestiniog Railway website for details.

WHO CAN APPLY
You need to be interested in the Vale of Ffestiniog way of life and the railway.

WHEN AND HOW TO APPLY
Apply to the Volunteer Officer of the Ffestiniog Railway.

SELECTION PROCESS
Recruitment and Selection processes vary – normally by letter or phone to the railway and a loose discussion of your aims and motivation.

TRAINING
For any job on the railway full training is always given.

SUPPORT FOR PARTICIPANTS
You will have the support of experienced volunteers.

Iona Community

The Iona Community is an ecumenical Christian movement whose Islands' work focuses around welcoming guests to join in its common life of work, worship and recreation. There are three Community centres on Iona and Mull: Iona Abbey and MacLeod centre on Iona, and Camas Adventure Centre on the Ross of Mull. Up to 35 volunteers work with the Community at any one time. Volunteers help from the beginning of March to the end of October, and may work as kitchen assistant, housekeeping assistant, maintenance assistant, general assistant, gardener, children's worker, church assistant, driver, shop assistant, front office assistant and, at Camas, as cook, maintenance assistant, gardener, art and craft worker or general assistant.

HOW LONG IT WILL LAST
You must be able to stay from six to 16 weeks. At Camas long-term 4–5-month posts are available. Some resident staff positions lasting from nine months to three years may be available.

WHERE YOU CAN GO
Iona or Mull.

PAYMENT
Full board and lodging and £25 a week pocket money.

THE COST TO YOU
Travel to Iona.

WHO CAN APPLY
You must be over 18 and fluent in English. People with first aid skills are particularly welcome. You do not have to be Christian but you are expected to attend a fair number of the services.

WHEN AND HOW TO APPLY
To Iona Abbey. The volunteer programme runs from the middle of March to the end of October.

SELECTION PROCESS
Applicants are not interviewed. You may be asked to complete a vetting form.

PLACEMENT
The Community will try to appoint you to your preferred job, but that might not always be possible.

TRAINING
No specific training is given.

SUPPORT FOR PARTICIPANTS
There are times to ask questions and share concerns.

The Ironbridge Gorge Museum

This museum was established to conserve the heritage of the Ironbridge Gorge and to interpret its history for future generations. Volunteers are involved in all aspects of the Museum's work. Volunteer work can involve acting as a site demonstrator, site maintenance volunteer, in the wardrobe department, guiding or other activities. There is no particular pro-gramme as such, but the Museum encourages students who are con-templating a career in the museum/tourism/leisure/heritage fields seriously to think about coming to work for it for a year. You should understand that you will be asked to do menial tasks as well as the more interesting ones.

HOW LONG IT WILL LAST
General, seasonal or up to a year.

WHERE YOU CAN GO
Shropshire.

PAYMENT
There are very rarely opportunities for paid work all the year round, but there are opportunities for well motivated students to work for the Museum on a seasonal basis between Easter and the end of October.

THE COST TO YOU
Accommodation, food, etc.

WHO CAN APPLY
You need good interpersonal skills and be adaptable.

WHEN AND HOW TO APPLY
Contact the Ironbridge Gorge Museum at the address at the back of the book.

SELECTION PROCESS
Applicants will be contacted.

PLACEMENT
You would work at the Museum.

TRAINING
Full training is given for site demonstrators and guides.

SUPPORT FOR PARTICIPANTS
You will have the support of the Museum staff and experienced volunteers.

£

The Leonard Cheshire Foundation

The Leonard Cheshire Foundation is a charitable trust presiding over 83 UK residential Cheshire Homes and over thirty Family Support Services for people suffering from a wide variety of disabling conditions. Most Homes are for severely physically disabled adults, but a small number are for mentally handicapped adults and those recovering from mental illness. Young people can be temporarily employed as Care Assistants assisting with the day-to-day personal care of disabled residents and helping in a wide variety of other ways.

HOW LONG IT WOULD LAST
From three to twelve months.

WHERE YOU CAN GO
There are homes in most parts of the UK except central London.

PAYMENT
Free board and lodging and weekly pocket money.

THE COST TO YOU
Travel and incidental costs.

WHO CAN APPLY
You must be over 18, and preference is given to people under 35 who plan to take up medical or social work as a career. Volunteers must be willing to work hard and be adaptable and punctual.

WHEN AND HOW TO APPLY
Contact the Foundation for an application form.

SELECTION PROCESS
Selection is at the discretion of the Foundation.

PLACEMENT
Employment in any particular Home cannot be guaranteed.

TRAINING
Any necessary on-the-job training will be provided.

SUPPORT FOR PARTICIPANTS
You will be supported by staff and other volunteers.

£ | London City Mission

This is an evangelistic organisation looking for voluntary evangelists to join the City Vision team and work in London City Mission Christian centres all over London. They work alongside full-time missionaries for one year. There are also shorter Summer Evangelism schemes lasting for two weeks. The work is varied and may involve door-to-door visits, open-air meetings, holiday clubs, children's clubs, coffee bars, practical work, work with the homeless, and church and centre work.

HOW LONG IT WILL LAST
City Vision: one year; Summer Evangelism scheme: two to four weeks.

WHERE YOU CAN GO
London.

PAYMENT
None.

THE COST TO YOU
City Vision: no charge but participants are encouraged to raise support. Summer Evangelism: £25 per week covering accommodation and everything you need to survive in London.

WHO CAN APPLY
People aged 18–30.

WHEN AND HOW TO APPLY
Contact London City Mission Special Projects Department for further details and application forms.

SELECTION PROCESS
You are asked for an application form and two references (including one from your church minister).

PLACEMENT
For City Vision you are placed at one of 32 centres throughout London.

TRAINING
Full training is incorporated into the City Vision scheme.

SUPPORT FOR PARTICIPANTS
Every volunteer works under the direction of a full-time City Missionary.

£–££ | The National Trust

The National Trust can offer a certain number of opportunities for long-term voluntary work experience. Work involves helping the Trust with countryside management such as wardening, forestry and conservation work, and tasks associated with the management of the Trust's built heritage, including work in National Trust houses, gardens, offices and on archaeological projects.

HOW LONG IT WILL LAST
You must be able to work for a minimum of six months.

WHERE YOU CAN GO
Properties throughout the UK.

PAYMENT
The Trust will either provide transport or pay standard mileage rates for volunteers driving their own vehicles on Trust business. Volunteers may also claim travel expenses for the interview and initially getting to their place of work. The Trust is sometimes able to provide shared self-catering accommodation for which you pay no rent but will contribute to telephone and electricity bills. The Trust provides any special footwear or clothing needed to meet health and safety regulations.

THE COST TO YOU
Accommodation (if the Trust cannot house you) and food.

WHO CAN APPLY
You should be 18 or over, and gap year students are welcome to apply.

WHEN AND HOW TO APPLY
Apply to the Trust.

SELECTION PROCESS
Your acceptance is subject to a satisfactory interview and one month's statutory probation period.

PLACEMENT
The final choice of workplace will depend on the Trust's needs and each volunteer's previous experience and qualifications.

TRAINING
The Trust will provide on-the-job training and possibly nationally recognised qualifications.

SUPPORT FOR PARTICIPANTS
You will be given the details of a member of staff to whom you are responsible and to whom you can turn for guidance.

Northern Ireland Volunteer Development Agency

The Agency provides advice and information on volunteer opportunities in Northern Ireland. It also aims to promote volunteering throughout Northern Ireland and provides a central resource of support, information and training for all those involving volunteers, whether voluntary organisations, statutory agencies, community or self-help groups.

£££££-£££££ | Ockenden International

Ockenden International aims to support refugees, displaced people and the disadvantaged at home and overseas. Its UK commitments include Kilmore House, a residential home for people with learning difficulties, physical disabilities and challenging behaviour, including a group of orphaned Vietnamese and Cambodians for whom it provides a home. Volunteers are needed and your work could include domestic work, driving and, most of all, helping residents to develop their abilities and self-confidence. There are no volunteer opportunities overseas.

HOW LONG IT WILL LAST
One year, although shorter appointments occur occasionally.

WHERE YOU CAN GO
The residential home, Kilmore House, is at Camberley, Surrey.

PAYMENT
As a Volunteer Support Worker you can claim up to £30 per week for personal expenses and free board and accommodation.

THE COST TO YOU
You will need your fare to Camberley.

WHO CAN APPLY
You must be over 18. A full driving licence is an advantage.

WHEN AND HOW TO APPLY
You can apply at any time, but most volunteers join in August and September. Contact the personnel officer for further information.

SELECTION PROCESS
Qualifications or experience are not usually necessary.

PLACEMENT
You work at Kilmore House.

TRAINING
This will be given on-the-job as necessary.

SUPPORT FOR PARTICIPANTS
There is a managerial team of three, and five further Senior Support workers as well as fifteen Support workers.

Royal Society for the Protection of Birds (RSPB)

The RSPB has a well-organised volunteering scheme, where it identifies the work needed, recruits a volunteer whose skills and interests match the task, and enters into a proper contract with the volunteer. The most popular form of this is the Voluntary Wardening Scheme. You must work for at least one week. First-time volunteers can work up to four weeks maximum. Longer periods of volunteering can be negotiated after this initial period. The RSPB may be able to arrange longer stints at some RSPB nature reserves as part of a portfolio of gap year opportunities. To find out whether the RSPB can provide you with the opportunity, contact the Youth and Volunteers Department at the RSPB.

SCADU (The National Centre for Student Volunteering in the Community)

SCADU exists to support, develop and promote student community action groups in the UK. They are set up to enable students to develop volunteering projects in partnership with their local communities. Volunteers devise their own projects and work with every possible group of people in the community. There are over 170 local Student Community Action (SCA) groups in the UK.

Once you get to university or college, you can join (or form) a SCA group. This would be a good way of continuing your gap year volunteering experience as well as gaining experience if you want to do community work before starting a job. SCAs are generally based in the student unions of universities and colleges of higher education. Individual SCAs vary in size and character, but they all aim to be a student-led body working in partnership with local people to devise projects that support immediate needs. SCADU provides help with training, publications, help for new and established groups, information, networking, and a mailing list.

£££££ Scripture Union

Scripture Union is a charity which encourages people of all ages in their knowledge and understanding of the Christian faith. The SU year-out scheme is called YeS You, and people over the age of 18 are placed with SU evangelists or schools workers around England and Wales. You get other experiences as well as leadership, theological and personal development training.

HOW LONG IT WILL LAST
Ten months.

WHERE YOU CAN GO
England and Wales.

PAYMENT
None.

THE COST TO YOU
You will be required to raise a maximum of £3500 sponsorship, and the SU will help you to do this.

WHO CAN APPLY
You must be aged over 18 and a Christian. You may have a particular skill such as music, drama or administration, although this is not vital.

WHEN AND HOW TO APPLY
Apply as soon as possible, preferably by July, before the September you want to start. Get an application form from the SU. You will need to supply references.

SELECTION PROCESS
You will be called for interview and your references taken up, and you and the SU together will then decide whether the application should be pursued further. You meet the SU worker you might work with, and then a final decision is made by you and the SU.

PLACEMENT
This depends on which SU workers are able to take on a YeS You worker. Consideration is given to what you want to achieve through the year.

TRAINING
You will be given an induction course and will receive further training from your SU worker, and Moorlands College, in Dorset, through their Elivate course.

SUPPORT FOR PARTICIPANTS
Your SU worker will be responsible for you throughout the year, and you will have the opportunity of meeting and working with other SU staff and associates from time to time.

£

SHAD Wandsworth

SHAD Wandsworth is a London-based user-led charity which recruits volunteer personal assistants to work for individuals with severe physical disabilities. Volunteers act as 'facilitators' to an individual disabled person (a 'User-Manager'), working solely under their direction to help them lead an independent life. You would work in teams of two or three on a rota basis to provide 24-hour facilitation. Volunteers are not care workers but are recruited for the use of their 'arms and legs'. The work varies according to the lifestyle of the disabled person, but will be explained before placement. Generally it includes personal care, household tasks and work or study facilitation.

HOW LONG IT WILL LAST
You would stay from four to six months.

WHERE YOU CAN GO
Wandsworth, London.

PAYMENT
You will get free accommodation and a weekly allowance of £60.

THE COST TO YOU
Travel and incidental expenses.

WHO CAN APPLY
You must be 18–30, physically fit and committed to equal opportunities. You must be prepared to be on call 24 hours a day. Most volunteers need to be competent drivers, so a driving licence is desirable, but there are some placements for non-drivers.

WHEN AND HOW TO APPLY
Recruitment takes place throughout the year. Complete a SHAD application form – all applications are responded to.

SELECTION PROCESS
If your application is successful you will be invited to interview, either on your own or as part of a group.

PLACEMENT
Once you have been selected as suitable to SHAD, you are matched to an individual User-Manager. There is a one-month's probation period. If there are any difficulties on either side during a placement, SHAD will, if appropriate, try to place you elsewhere in the organisation or with another SHAD in London.

TRAINING
You will get formal manual handling/lifting training and receive disability awareness training on-the-job .

SUPPORT FOR PARTICIPANTS
SHAD Wandsworth have a full-time Volunteer Support Worker who offers both formal and informal support throughout your placement.

£

The Shaftsbury Society

The Shaftsbury Society is a charity that provides care and support services to people with specific needs such as people with learning and/or physical disabilities, and those who are homeless, poor or lonely. It has contacts with many different public sector organisations, and works with local churches. It runs over 60 services, including residential care homes. Some of the units take on volunteers and students.

HOW LONG IT WILL LAST
Arrange your commitment with the unit you apply to.

WHERE YOU CAN GO
The Shaftsbury Society operates across England. Where you can apply to will depend on which units have needs for volunteers.

PAYMENT
None.

THE COST TO YOU
If you want to volunteer for a unit away from home, you will need to find your living expenses and accommodation.

WHO CAN APPLY
The Society often takes on gap students in many units. Usually there is no criteria for applying, but it helps if you have an interest in the caring field and a good attitude to work.

WHEN AND HOW TO APPLY
Contact central office and you will be sent a list of units which take on volunteers and students. You should make your own arrangements with the units themselves.

SELECTION PROCESS
This is up to the individual units.

PLACEMENT
You can only apply to units which are actively seeking volunteers.

TRAINING
Any necessary training will be given on-the-job.

SUPPORT FOR PARTICIPANTS
You will receive support from the unit's staff.

£

The Simon Community

This is a community of homeless people and volunteers living and working with London's street homeless. The Community provides streetwork, soup and clothes runs around central London, a nightshelter, three houses and an office. Volunteers live as part of the Community and become involved in the many tasks necessary to the running of the Community. This might include, for example, streetwork, tea-runs, clothes-runs, driving, administration, cooking, cleaning, fundraising, campaigning or whatever else needs doing.

HOW LONG IT WILL LAST
You must commit for three months minimum, although six months or more is preferred.

WHERE YOU CAN GO
London.

PAYMENT
You live in a Community house and share meals and household chores.

THE COST TO YOU
Travel and other expenses.

WHO CAN APPLY
You must be at least 19.

WHEN AND HOW TO APPLY
To the Simon Community, at any time.

SELECTION PROCESS
A decision on whether to accept you will be made during the weekend (48 hours) all prospective workers are asked to spend with the Community.

PLACEMENT
Workers are assigned to a particular project but may be required to move to another project, depending on the Community's needs.

TRAINING
During the weekend you will take part in Community activity and decide whether it is what you want to do. Internal and external training are available.

SUPPORT FOR PARTICIPANTS
There is an emphasis on individual and group support.

£££ Time For God (TFG)

TFG aims to provide young people with opportunities to explore the Christian discipleship through voluntary service. The scheme is ecumenical and is sponsored by most of the Church denominations. Placements vary but typically can include residential care homes, working with the homeless or drug addicts, churches, hostels, youth projects, conference or outdoor pursuit centres.

HOW LONG IT WILL LAST
Volunteers serve for eight to twelve months.

WHERE YOU WILL GO
UK

PAYMENT
Board and lodging (or payment for meals if not provided) and pocket money, out-of-pocket expenses and fares home.

THE COST TO YOU
There is a registration fee. You will also need to raise £500 for training conferences and support, split between the applicant and the home church.

WHO CAN APPLY
You do not need any specific qualifications but must be Christian and between 18 and 25.

WHEN AND HOW TO APPLY
Write or telephone for a TFG application pack. Fill it in and supply three references on the forms provided and four passport photos.

SELECTION PROCESS
Your referees will be contacted and TFG may contact you. If this proves satisfactory you will be accepted, but this does not guarantee a placement. You then attend a briefing day.

PLACEMENT
You will be matched to a suitable placement. If both you and the placement agree, you can prepare for an exploratory visit. If you are not satisfied with the placement at any time, another will be found for you.

TRAINING
TFG provides three residential training courses for volunteers which take place at the beginning, middle and end of their service. The sessions last two or three days. In addition, the placement will provide any training required specific to your post.

SUPPORT FOR PARTICIPANTS
You will get on-the spot support from the placement in the form of managerial support directly related to the work. You will also have a TFG 'friend' outside the immediate work situation in whom you can confide. A TFG field worker will visit each volunteer and TFG staff are on call to deal with any unforeseen problems or difficulties.

Voluntary Service Belfast (VSB)

VSB is the Volunteer Bureau for Belfast. Its role is to support individuals who wish to volunteer by putting them in touch with local community and voluntary organisations. Help is given to a wide variety of groups including older people, children, families, environmental and conservation projects. Young people who are interested in team-building, gaining skills and personal development and community service can take part in either the Long Term Volunteer (LTV) programme or Prince's Trust Volunteer programme.

HOW LONG IT WILL LAST
LTVs must be able to commit themselves for six months full-time. PTVs must commit to 12 weeks full-time.

WHERE YOU CAN GO
Greater Belfast.

PAYMENT
There is no payment for either scheme. LTVs get a meal allowance and travel expenses. PTVs receive travel expenses or childcare expenses.

THE COST TO YOU
It is assumed you are living in Belfast.

WHO CAN APPLY
Any young person aged between 16–25 years can apply.

WHEN AND HOW TO APPLY
To VSB. Telephone or call in person to receive an information pack.

SELECTION PROCESS
This is based on your application form and an interview.

PLACEMENT
LTVs are placed in VSB departments and also with a community organis-ation. PTVs take part in a wide variety of activities and will identify, plan and execute projects with the help of a team leader.

TRAINING
LTVs are offered a wide variety of personal development and accredited training courses. Recognition for training can also be gained through Millennium Volunteer Awards. Prince's Trust programmes cover team-building, computing, first aid, jobsearch skills and a community placement. PTVs also work towards NVQ keyskills and OCR accreditation.

SUPPORT FOR PARTICIPANTS
All young people are supported by VSB staff who provide ongoing guid-ance and supervision. Prince's Trust Volunteers are assigned to a group with a team leader who supervises and supports.

World Service Enquiry

World Service Enquiry provides information and advice to people who want to work, volunteer or travel in the Third World. It covers all skills, areas and faiths. It produces an annual guide giving lots of information about opportunities and where to find out more. The back pages list organisations who specifically take volunteers on short-term placements. The booklet is free and available by post (send an SAE for 40p with A5 envelope – a £2.50 donation to publication costs is suggested) or can be downloaded from the World Service Enquiry website.

Under its other title, Christians Abroad, World Service Enquiry recruits and places qualified Christians overseas in the developing world with partner organisations.

Youth for Britain

This organisation provides a Worldwide Volunteering Database, on disk, of over 250,000 annual placements for young people, many of them suitable for gap year students. It details over 800 organisations with projects throughout the UK and in 214 countries worldwide. It is a computer-based guidance system. The database can be accessed through schools, careers officers, etc, or through YFB's own postal enquiry service should the database not be available locally. Some libraries may also have the database. Projects range from one week to a year. Some schemes will pay all your expenses and some pocket money; others will require you to raise costs of several hundred pounds. Applicants must be between 16 and 25.

You enter personal criteria such as age, type of placement sought, location and start of project, time available, financial and any disability considerations, etc. These are matched within seconds on the database records. Addresses and information about all appropriate organisations are then shown on screen and can be printed out. You must satisfy yourself about the project before starting on it.

SEE ALSO:

BTCV, *page 121*;   Oasis, *page 107*;

Crusoe, *page 93*;   Tear Fund, *page 113*

6

VOLUNTARY AND COMMUNITY WORK ABROAD

Voluntary and community work schemes abroad require commitment from you; they usually also require money. Opportunities range from teaching English to children to practical environmental projects.

There is a fine line to be drawn between voluntary work and some paid work overseas. Some overseas voluntary work will give you a little pocket money – some paid work gives you no more than that. The difference is that voluntary work requires you to fund yourself for the duration. You may be given help with free accommodation and food, but often not.

You should be keen to do the work involved. You will have fun, but the main purpose is to help with whatever project you attend. The people you are helping are usually not very well off and your skills mean a lot to them. If you stop and go home half-way through, or do not pull your weight, you will damage both the project and relations with that community.

Like the UK voluntary schemes, many are run by religious organisations. Check whether they ask participants to be from a particular religious group or whether they accept people of all beliefs and none.

For most voluntary work abroad you need nothing except stamina, enthusiasm and a willingness to take part to the best of your ability. Occasionally you will need a basic knowledge of a foreign language.

Most voluntary work requires you to be at least 18, although a few projects will take you at 17. Some are particularly geared towards gap year students. (Also see chapter 3.)

For some projects you will have to raise living costs and air fares, which can run to a thousand pounds or more. Costs might also include registration with the scheme, board and lodging, specialist clothing and equipment, insurance, and a specialist course (e.g. language course). Include the cost of an up-to-date full passport if you do not already have one, and some more exotic vaccinations if these are needed in certain areas. You may need to budget for travel to and from the project and the airport, and living expenses when you are there.

Many project organisers are aware that the costs can be prohibitive and give advice about raising money through sponsorship and other schemes.

You are doing something worthwhile and getting to know the people and country at first hand and not as a tourist. As part of the community you get to find out what life is really like for people in another country.

The disadvantages are that you may be on your own or with only one other British volunteer a long way from home. There will be someone to keep in touch with you, but it can be lonely and you may feel homesick at first. You won't be living in the lap of luxury either and must be prepared to rough it in sometimes very primitive conditions. This can be depressing if you are not used to it or not prepared to enter into the spirit of the thing. Not being able to speak the language can make you feel isolated too, although people will try to be friendly. You may also feel unsure about doing the work you are asked to do – for example, standing up in front of a class of secondary school children and trying to teach them some English can be nerve-wracking if you have no previous experience.

However, people who complete their projects usually find that they return more confident, having enjoyed a unique and valuable experience.

Many projects will provide you with accommodation, but if you have to find your own there are a number of options. You could check at the local college or university, if there is one, about the availability of student accommodation; you could camp if a suitable site is available; you could ask the project leader to find a family for you to stay with; if the project is taking place in a building, you could ask to sleep in the hall or a spare room. The project leader should be able to give you advice and help with finding accommodation if necessary. Once you are there, you could get together with other volunteers to rent rooms or a house for the duration of your stay. Don't forget that if you are arranging your own accommodation you will need to take money to pay for this.

££££-£££££ | African Conservation Experience

This organisation provides students with the opportunity to do conservation work on game and nature reserves in Southern Africa. Students work side by side with conservationists and rangers on a wide range of conservation and research projects.

HOW LONG IT WILL LAST
One to three months.

WHERE YOU CAN GO
Reserves throughout Southern Africa.

PAYMENT
None.

THE COST TO YOU
The cost varies at reserves but example costs are: Kagga Kamma £1795 (4 weeks) and £2275 (12 weeks); Shamwari Game Reserve between £2350 and £2935. This includes flights, transfers and full board.

WHO CAN APPLY
School-leavers, undergraduates and graduates – any young person between the age of 18 and 30 something who is young at heart and enthusiastic about conservation and the environment.

WHEN AND HOW TO APPLY
Contact African Conservation Experience for details.

SELECTION PROCESS
You attend an Introductory and Assessment Weekend at an Adventure Centre to assess your suitability for one of the limited number of placements.

PLACEMENT
The placement is decided by discussion between ACE and the student.

TRAINING
None required. Some training may be given at the reserve.

SUPPORT FOR PARTICIPANTS
Experienced conservationists appointed by the reserves are responsible for you during your entire time on the reserve. The Coordinator on the reserve is the point of contact for allocation of work projects, to act as tutor/mentor and listen to any problems you may have.

£££££
AFS International Youth Development

AFS is an international, voluntary, non-governmental, non-profit organisation that provides intercultural learning opportunities. It offers two opportunities to take part in an intercultural experience. The *Schools Programme* is for the age range 15–18 to spend a year living in another country. Students live with a volunteer host family as a member of that family, attend a local school and become involved in community life. The *International Volunteer Programme* is for people aged 18–29 to spend six months abroad helping with a social project. You live with a volunteer host family and work alongside local people on community initiatives in the fields of environment, health, education, sanitation, agriculture, community education and development, women's issues, drug education and rehabilitation, and with underprivileged children, people with disabilities and the elderly.

HOW LONG IT WILL LAST
Schools Programme – 10 months. *International Volunteer Programme* – six months.

WHERE YOU CAN GO
Schools Programme placements are in 18 different countries. For the *International Volunteer Programme* you go to Brazil, Ecuador, Honduras, South Africa, Venezuela, Guatemala or Peru.

PAYMENT
None.

THE COST TO YOU
The fee for *Schools Programme* students is about £3950, although some grants may be available for part of the fee. Advice is given about fundraising. The fee covers travel to and from the UK, travel within the host country, full medical insurance, orientation camps and language support, support network and counselling, 24-hour emergency cover in the UK and host country, and administration in both countries. You may also need to find money for a visa or for medical certificates, etc, depending on the country. You will also need pocket money: £500 minimum is suggested for the year. For *International Volunteer Programme* students the fee is about £2950.

WHO CAN APPLY
Schools Programme students must be between 15 and 18 and a full-time student. You do not need to know the language.

Applicants must have been in full-time education from 17 and be aged 18–29 to go on the *International Volunteer Programme*.

WHEN AND HOW TO APPLY
For both schemes you should complete the application form available from AFS and return it with a fee of £10. Applications for *International Volunteer Programme* can be accepted at any time of the year but preferably at least six months before departure in January/February or July. *Schools Programme* departures are in July, August or September and you should apply by the previous 31 October.

SELECTION PROCESS
The Selection process has two stages: a selection meeting/interview and family visit by a volunteer, and acceptance of the completed final application forms by the host country. Depending on the number of people who apply from your area, you will either be invited to a regional selection meeting or arrangements will be made to interview you at home.

PLACEMENT
Time and care is taken to place *Schools Programme* students with a suitable family who will arrange for you to attend the local school. *Schools Programme* applicants state their preferences for country and AFS uses its knowledge of the countries to make the best match for the applicant. There is a range of about 15 countries available each year. For the *International*

Volunteer Programme candidates can choose from four countries where they want to go.

TRAINING
International Volunteer Service students are given an intensive course of language tuition during the first month of the programme. Typically you will be given 40 to 80 hours of tuition, depending on the country. AFS also provide learning materials before the programme starts.

SUPPORT FOR PARTICIPANTS
You will be put in touch with a local person whom you can contact with any problems, queries or just for a chat. Each country has professional staff on call 24 hours a day to help you.

££-£££

Australian Trust for Conservation Volunteers (ATCV)

ATCV has offices in all Australian States and Territories and completes around 1200 projects per year. Projects take place all over Australia, but placements depend on availability in any State or Territory. The projects involve practical conservation work. Typical projects include tree planting, weed control, seed collection, erosion and salinity control, building and painting walking tracks, historic building restoration, flora and fauna surveys and monitoring, and habitat restoration. Volunteers work from 8am to 4pm Monday to Friday, and part of the weekend is spent travelling to the next project.

HOW LONG IT WILL LAST
Four weeks to five months.

WHERE YOU CAN GO
All States of Australia, including some remote locations.

PAYMENT
None.

THE COST TO YOU
You might pay $20 per day for short placements or about $8 per day if you agree to stay for 20 weeks. You will need to find your air fare to Australia and have a visitor's visa and medical insurance.

WHO CAN APPLY
No special skills are required, but you should be reasonably fit.

WHEN AND HOW TO APPLY
Projects run all year and applications are accepted at any time. Write to ATCV for a form.

SELECTION PROCESS
None.

PLACEMENT
Volunteers are placed on projects in the States requested, depending on availability.

TRAINING
ATCV provides all training necessary to complete a project.

SUPPORT FOR PARTICIPANTS
You get all meals, accommodation and transport to projects. You must make your own arrangements to get to the ATCV office in the State of your placement.

££-£££££

Baptist Missionary Society – Youth Action Teams

The Baptist Missionary Society works with Christians in over thirty countries. Youth Action Teams are teams of young people sent all over the world by the Society for a year. Teams get involved in a wide variety of activities, from evangelistic events to teaching, social care, youth work and practical tasks such as painting churches. The year starts with a six-week training period followed by six months overseas working alongside BMS missionaries or partner churches. On returning to the UK in April there is a short debriefing and preparation time before teams embark on a two-month tour of the UK sharing their experiences with Baptist Churches. The year ends in June.

BMS also runs Summer Teams that do similar work but which only go overseas for between two to six weeks, and also UK Action Teams.

HOW LONG IT WILL LAST
The Youth Action Teams year runs from September to June. Summer Teams operate during July or August.

WHERE YOU CAN GO
Teams go to countries in Asia, Africa, Europe and Central and South America.

PAYMENT
None.

THE COST TO YOU
You will need to find about £2900 towards the cost of training, travel, food and accommodation, etc. Summer Teams cost from £350 to £1500. Help is available from a number of sources and BMS would not turn an applicant down on financial grounds.

WHO CAN APPLY
You must be Christian and aged between 18 and 25.

WHEN AND HOW TO APPLY

You can obtain information at any time of year. The application process begins in November; a pre-selection weekend and interviews are held in March.

SELECTION PROCESS

Selection is by application form, pre-selection weekend and interview.

PLACEMENT

BMS church partners in other countries request teams and offer to host them. Usually countries will have a team every two years. BMS then put teams together and assign them to overseas destinations. Many factors are taken into account when deciding which applicants are best suited to a particular country and team. The decision is made by the panel of people who first interviewed the candidates.

TRAINING

Youth Action Teams get six weeks of training involving devotional, educational and practical training on a wide variety of subjects and a week's placement at a UK church.

SUPPORT FOR PARTICIPANTS

There is a hierarchy of pastoral support. Team members can turn first to the individual (or couple) in pastoral charge, who is either a BMS missionary or another person appointed by the church with which the team is working. Next there are BMS regional representatives and also a Volunteers Manager based at Didcot who is responsible for overseeing the Action Team scheme and is in regular contact with the teams by e-mail/letter. Finally there is the BMS General Director, who is the final authority for major problems or disciplinary action.

£££ Camphill Village USA Inc

This is part of the Camphill Village movement (see chapter 5). Camphill USA has about 75–100 volunteers from all over the world throughout the year and participating in its foundation year program. This Village is a community in which life is shared with 110 adults aged 24–82 with mental disabilities. It has an extensive farm and garden and operates eight craft shops. Volunteers help with all aspects of life in the Community.

HOW LONG IT WILL LAST

The preferred length of commitment is from six to twelve months.

WHERE YOU CAN GO

Camphill Village, Copake, NY, USA.

PAYMENT

You get $75 per month pocket money and $440 at the end of twelve months' stay towards a three-week holiday. Camphill provide Letters of Invitation (B-1), J-1 or F-1 visas, depending on circumstances.

THE COST TO YOU
Travel to USA.

WHO CAN APPLY
You must be in good health, physically mobile and able to speak English.

WHEN AND HOW TO APPLY
Contact the Associate Director.

SELECTION PROCESS
Initial selection is based on your application.

PLACEMENT
You will work at Copake.

TRAINING
There is a first-year foundation/introductory year training.

SUPPORT FOR PARTICIPANTS
Support comes from within the Community.

£££££

CMJ (The Church's Ministry among Jewish People)

CMJ is a Christian society ministering to people in Israel. CMJ has several guest houses/worship centres in Israel. Volunteers stay at the centres and help with reception and domestic and maintenance duties.

HOW LONG IT WILL LAST
Three to twelve months, starting at a variety of times.

WHERE YOU CAN GO
Israel – Isfiya near Haifa, Tel Aviv or Jerusalem.

PAYMENT
Pocket money is provided if necessary.

THE COST TO YOU
You must find your own air fare and medical insurance. Once in Israel, CMJ provides your board and keep.

WHO CAN APPLY
You must be 18–80, in good health, a fully committed Christian and involved in your local church.

WHEN AND HOW TO APPLY
Apply to CMJ six months before you intend to go.

SELECTION PROCESS
You must complete application forms and provide references from a friend, tutor or employer, minister or vicar.

PLACEMENT
At Haifa or one of CMJ's centres.

TRAINING
You receive information before departure and training in Israel.

SUPPORT FOR PARTICIPANTS
You are encouraged to receive support from your home church/congregation and will receive close supervision and pastoral support from centre managers, many of whom have trained in pastoral work.

£££££ | Concordia

Concordia is a small, non-profit charity that has been involved in international youth exchange since 1943. Concordia is committed to promoting international voluntary work for 18–30 year olds as an educational and cultural experience. Volunteers work as part of an international team on international volunteer projects (IVPs) involving social work and children's playschemes. Concordia also organises longer-term places on farm schemes in Switzerland and Norway.

HOW LONG IT WILL LAST
IVPs last from two to three weeks, with the main season from June to September, though some winter/spring projects are available. Farm schemes last from three to six months.

WHERE YOU CAN GO
The UK, East, West and Central Europe, Japan, North Africa, the Middle East and the USA.

PAYMENT
None for IVPs, but food and accommodation are provided free of charge. Farm schemes provide pocket money.

THE COST TO YOU
IVPs volunteers pay a registration fee of £75 (£50 for projects in the UK) and fund their own travel. Board and accommodation are provided.

WHO CAN APPLY
Eighteen–30 year olds. Generally the work doesn't require specific skills or experience, though real motivation is a must. Some social projects may require language skills. Volunteers applying for Japan, Morocco or Tunisia must be 20+. Limited places are available to 17 year olds in Germany and France.

WHEN AND HOW TO APPLY
For more information volunteers should write enclosing a SAE. Details of summer projects will be available from April. Applications are taken from April onwards. Volunteers wishing to receive a programme should write enclosing a cheque for £3 (clearly indicating return address) to the Volunteer Programme Manager at the address given.

SELECTION PROCESS

Concordia places volunteers on their chosen projects according to availability and therefore requests volunteers to list a number of choices on application. Some placements require specific motivation or skills, in which case the most suitably qualified applicant will be placed.

PLACEMENT

Concordia refers applications to its partner organisations internationally, who organise and coordinate your placement.

TRAINING

This will depend on the project – usually on-the-job.

SUPPORT FOR PARTICIPANTS

Local project co-ordinators are on hand 24 hours a day to deal with day-to-day problems.

££££

Crusoe

Crusoe (Crusaders Overseas Expeditions) is part of the Crusader organisation, which trains and teaches young people in the Christian faith. World Crusoe teams consist of up to twelve members of both sexes, headed by male and female leaders, which get the chance to live and work in a developing country.

HOW LONG IT WILL LAST

World Crusoe projects last four weeks.

WHERE YOU CAN GO

Recent teams have been to Central America, Chile, Kenya, Romania, Thailand and Uganda.

PAYMENT

None.

THE COST TO YOU

£1300, excluding the cost of the orientation weekend and travel in the UK.

WHO CAN APPLY

You must be between 16 and 22 and a committed Christian.

WHEN AND HOW TO APPLY

Complete an application form and you will then be invited to attend a residential orientation weekend.

SELECTION PROCESS

At an orientation weekend the team leaders will assess you, and successful candidates will be offered a place on a team.

PLACEMENT

If candidates express a preference for a particular project, this is taken into account when forming the teams.

TRAINING

The work is likely to be of a fairly unskilled and practical nature.

SUPPORT FOR PARTICIPANTS

At all times maximum care is taken in terms of safety and health precautions.

££££

Experience Exchange Programme

The Experience Exchange Programme is run by the United Society for the Propagation of the Gospel (USPG) – a mission agency of the Anglican Church and the Methodist Church. The Experience Exchange Programme enables people to spend time living and working alongside local people in church-based projects such as schools, community development programmes or hostels.

HOW LONG IT WILL LAST

Between six and twelve months.

WHERE YOU CAN GO

Africa, Asia, South America, Eastern Europe or the Caribbean.

PAYMENT

None, although the church or placement overseas often provides board and lodging. USPG is sometimes able to make small grants towards the cost of a placement.

THE COST TO YOU

You will need to raise about £2500 for living expenses, pocket money, air fare and any other travel. A small fee is charged for an Exploration Weekend before application.

WHO CAN APPLY

You must be over 18 and attached to a home church in Britain.

WHEN AND HOW TO APPLY

You are advised to attend an Exploration Weekend. If you are still interested after the weekend you will be invited to apply, and if there might be a place for you, you will be invited to a selection day.

SELECTION PROCESS

Selection is done in stages from the time your application is received to having a one-to-one interview.

PLACEMENT

USPG will try to match your skills and interests to an appropriate placement.

TRAINING

You are offered training before going on your placement.

SUPPORT FOR PARTICIPANTS
You will be supported by your home church and the receiving church over-seas.

EIL

The EIL arranges many programmes of interest to gap year students wanting to spend time abroad (see also chapter 4). It also organises a European Voluntary Service (EVS) initiative which is funded by the European Commission. This enables EIL to recruit volunteers to work on a variety of projects in Europe, working with the disabled, for example, on environmental or conservation projects or youth service for a year, at a variety of locations.

HOW LONG IT WILL LAST
Six or 12 months.

WHERE YOU CAN GO
Europe, generally in Greece, Italy, France and Spain.

PAYMENT
You will get language training, weekly pocket money, accommodation and board for the programme year, insurance, and your UK return flight.

THE COST TO YOU
None.

WHO CAN APPLY
You must be between 18 and 25, with skills appropriate to your place-ment. Some knowledge of a relevant European language is helpful but not essential.

WHEN AND HOW TO APPLY
Contact EIL for information and details of application procedure.

SELECTION PROCESS
Applications are accepted on a first come, first served basis.

PLACEMENT
This will be agreed between you and EIL.

TRAINING
You will get a two-week relevant language course pre-placement.

SUPPORT FOR PARTICIPANTS
You will receive support and guidance throughout your year from a pro-gramme coordinator, and three evaluations during the year.

£

Friends of Israel Educational Trust – Bridge in Britain

Bridge in Britain is an annual scholarship programme sponsored by a British Foundation, the Friends of Israel Educational Trust. The scheme is designed to promote knowledge and understanding of the problems and achievements of the State of Israel and its peoples. Up to twelve school-leavers are offered passage to Israel and free board and lodging for five creative months in Israel. Under the scheme, award winners are offered a working place on a kibbutz, two months' community service in a development town, work in a northern Israel *moshav* (smallholders' co-operative), seminars and organised tours, as well as free time to travel. You can take part in an archaeological dig as an optional extra at your own expense.

HOW LONG IT WILL LAST
Six months.

WHERE YOU CAN GO
Israel.

PAYMENT
None.

THE COST TO YOU
Spending money – the suggested figure for six months is £600. The scholarship covers board and lodging for five months of the half year away.

WHO CAN APPLY
You must be a school-leaver aged 18–19, in good health and a UK resident. No knowledge of Hebrew or Arabic is required. Places are open to all, regardless of sex, religion, race or creed. You need to be keen to learn about new people and places and prepared for a demanding programme.

WHEN AND HOW TO APPLY
Apply by 1 July. You must submit an essay of at least 400 words explaining why you want to spend time in Israel, a handwritten covering letter, a CV, details of interests and future plans, two passport photos and two references – one academic, one personal. The programme starts in the January after acceptance.

SELECTION PROCESS
Shortlisted candidates are interviewed individually.

TRAINING
You will get a pre-departure briefing by experts and past award winners, and on-site support and help from coordinators at every stage.

SUPPORT FOR PARTICIPANTS
Coordinators will be available for back-up throughout the period in Israel.

££

Habitat for Humanity International (HFHI)

This is a non-profit, Christian housing ministry dedicated to eliminating substandard housing from the world. Individuals form HFHI affiliate groups in their communities and work together to build houses for people who could not otherwise afford decent shelter. HFHI has built over 50,000 houses worldwide in over fifty countries.

HFHI cannot place people directly at its affiliates. If you hope to spend your entire gap year with HFHI, you will probably take part in construction or administrative work at their headquarters in Americus, Georgia, USA. You are responsible for obtaining your own visa. However, on acceptance, HFHI can provide documentation that may help you in obtaining the necessary visa. This could be done by arranging sponsorship via an organisation such as a church. Contact the UK branch, Habitat for Humanity Great Britain, who can help you apply to the HFHI Americus project.

HOW LONG IT WILL LAST
You could spend your gap year with HFHI.

WHERE YOU CAN GO
Americus, Georgia, USA.

PAYMENT
None, but you get a food stipend and volunteer housing.

THE COST TO YOU
Transport, visa and insurance.

WHO CAN APPLY
You must be 18 or older, have commitment and uphold Christian principles.

WHEN AND HOW TO APPLY
Contact Habitat for Humanity Great Britain for information about how to apply to Americus. They can also give you information about short-term HFH volunteering opportunities in the UK or abroad.

SELECTION PROCESS
The Selection process is competitive. Completed applications are reviewed to fill positions at HFHI headquarters.

PLACEMENT
This is dependent on what positions are available at HFHI headquarters. A representative will be in touch with you regarding placement once your completed application has been received.

TRAINING
Many positions require specific skills, but if accepted volunteers will receive any necessary training on-the-job .

SUPPORT FOR PARTICIPANTS
You will have a supervisor to provide professional and personal advice. There is a Human Resources department to provide organisational back-up, including a manager dedicated to the welfare of volunteers.

£££££ Health Projects Abroad (HPA)

HPA offers you the chance to live in rural Tanzania working with other young people and local villagers on a community development project, such as building a primary school or health centre. All projects are part of long-term development programmes and are meeting a real need for the local people.

HOW LONG IT WILL LAST
Three months.

WHERE YOU CAN GO
Tanzania.

PAYMENT
None.

THE COST TO YOU
£3000, including your flight.

WHO CAN APPLY
You must be 18+ at the time of departure.

WHEN AND HOW TO APPLY
Departures are late April, late June or late August. Extending your stay for independent post-project travel is encouraged. Contact HPA for an application pack.

SELECTION PROCESS
On the basis of your application form you will invited to attend a selection weekend in Derbyshire. The weekend consists of a series of short tasks undertaken in teams of five or six. At the end of the weekend a team will be chosen to go to Tanzania.

PLACEMENT
There is no choice as to the projects, but you can choose which time of year you want to go.

TRAINING
HPA has received a National training award for its training and support before, during and after your project. You attend two intensive training weekends. Advice on fund-raising skills are included.

SUPPORT FOR PARTICIPANTS

You will be in regular contact with the UK office team and will spend time with returned volunteers throughout your pre-departure time. On your return you take part in a follow-up weekend.

£££–££££ Indian Volunteers for Community Service (IVCS)

IVCS organises a DRIVE scheme that provides an opportunity for anyone over 18 to stay in a village project in India, experience a different culture, learn about development work and possibly become actively involved.

HOW LONG IT WILL LAST

You can spend up to six months living in a rural development project in India. The minimum length of stay is three weeks.

WHERE YOU CAN GO

You spend the first three weeks in a project in North India. Afterwards there are opportunities to go on projects scattered throughout India.

PAYMENT

None.

THE COST TO YOU

You will finance your own visit, including air fares, food and accommodation, and local sightseeing. You must become an IVCS member, costing £15 per annum. There is a placement fee of £160 which includes printed material, one-day orientation in London and three weeks' orientation in North India. This includes Hindi lessons, food and lodging.

WHO CAN APPLY

You must be over 18 and in good health.

WHEN AND HOW TO APPLY

Send a SAE to IVCS or download an application form from the IVCS website and send it with £15. You will be invited for a formal interview, which usually takes place in London. If successful, you make a payment to cover the cost of the first three weeks in India and an orientation day in London.

SELECTION PROCESS

The interview is a chance for IVCS and you to decide whether the scheme is right for you. There is a compulsory one-day orientation in London and for three weeks in India. If either you or the IVCS decide at this stage that you should not go on the scheme, the remaining three weeks' orientation fee will be refunded.

PLACEMENT

During the 21-day acclimatisation period you can decide which of the numerous projects you wish to visit. The choice of project depends on personal interests and is carried out in consultation with the IVCS Field Director or deputy at the home base project.

TRAINING
One-day orientation in London, three weeks' orientation in India, but no formal training.

SUPPORT FOR PARTICIPANTS
IVCS in the UK provides help and advice. While you are in India the project base where all applicants do their orientation will be your homebase throughout your stay.

£-££

International Voluntary Service (IVS)

IVS is a membership organisation that aims to promote peace, justice and understanding through voluntary work. Its main activity is to send volunteers on short-term voluntary work projects, called *international workcamps*. These are organised in conjunction with related and partnership organisations. Each workcamp takes between six and twenty participants who work together on a community project, for example, conservation projects, working with children, the elderly and with people with special needs. People under 18 can apply to UK workcamps only, with parental permission.

HOW LONG IT WILL LAST
Workcamps last from two to four weeks. After workcamp participation there are some opportunities for medium-term positions. Workcamps take place mainly between June and September, with a few in Winter and Spring.

WHERE YOU CAN GO
Workcamps take place in Europe, North Africa and the USA.

PAYMENT
None.

THE COST TO YOU
You must pay your own way and make your own way to the workcamp, where food and accommodation will be provided. Membership of IVS costs £15 for students.

WHO CAN APPLY
Anyone aged 18+ can apply, regardless of age, race, disability, or professional qualifications. Particular skills are not required.

WHEN AND HOW TO APPLY
You can buy a booklet, available from April, giving details of summer international workcamps. Contact the IVS for details. Volunteers with a disability are asked to tell IVS when they apply. If you live in Northern Ireland contact IVS-NI, which is an independent organisation (details on page 101).

SELECTION
The Selection process is informal and anyone is accepted. You can offer up to six preferences: your application is sent to the project for final selection. Some selection is made on the basis of nationality to ensure a good mix.

PLACEMENT
You make your own choice of project. Every effort is made to place you with the workcamp you choose, but certain workcamps may not be accessible for certain disabilities.

TRAINING
Training is an integral part of workcamp participation. There is sometimes the opportunity to take part in an orientation weekend if you wish.

SUPPORT FOR PARTICIPANTS
You will be given emergency contact numbers and addresses for IVS and the coordinator in the partnership organisation that is running your workcamp.

£-££

International Voluntary Service – Northern Ireland (IVS-NI)

IVS-NI is the Northern Irish branch of Service Civil International (SCI). SCI is an international non-governmental organisation committed to the promotion of peace and understanding through voluntary activities. SCI has 34 branches and groups in Asia, Australia, Europe and United States and approximately 10,000 active members and volunteers. SCI also works with partner organisations in countries in Eastern Europe, including the former Soviet Union, Africa and Latin America.

IVS-NI is a membership organisation and its main activity is to send volunteers on short-term voluntary work projects, called *international workcamps.* These are organised in conjunction with its branches and partnership organisations and provide an opportunity to explore the potential of an international group living together, to work, have fun and spark community action. Each workcamp takes between six and twenty participants who work together on a community project – for example anti-racist and ethnic minority work, third world solidarity projects, conservation projects, working with children, the elderly and with people with special needs. There are also limited places available on the Asian/African exchange programme, medium-term vacancies and IVS-NI is also involved in the European Voluntary Service programme, which is an EU-funded programme for young people aged between 18 and 25.

HOW LONG IT WILL LAST
Workcamps last from two to four weeks. After workcamp participation

there are some opportunities for medium-term positions. Workcamps take place mainly between June and September, with a few in Winter and Spring. Medium-term positions can last from two months to a year. The EVS programme lasts from six months to one year and is available in all EU countries plus Norway.

WHERE YOU CAN GO
Workcamps take place in Britain, Europe, the former Soviet Union, North Africa, Japan and the USA.

PAYMENT
None.

THE COST TO YOU
A few workcamps organised by IVS-NI partners may have a charge – apply to IVS-NI for prices. You must pay your own way and make your own way to the workcamp, where food and accommodation will be provided. Membership of IVS-NI costs £35 for students and the low waged, £55 for the employed.

WHO CAN APPLY
Anyone over 18 can apply, regardless of age, race, disability, or professional qualifications. Particular skills are not required.

WHEN AND HOW TO APPLY
Contact IVS-NI.

SELECTION
The Selection process is informal and anyone is accepted. You can offer up to six preferences: your application is sent to the project for final selection. Some selection is made on the basis of nationality to ensure a good mix.

PLACEMENT
You make your own choice of project. Every effort is made to place you with the workcamp you choose, but certain workcamps may not be accessible for certain disabilities.

TRAINING
Training is an integral part of workcamp participation. There is sometimes the opportunity to take part in an orientation weekend if you wish.

SUPPORT FOR PARTICIPANTS
You will be given emergency contact numbers and addresses for IVS-NI and the coordinator in the partnership organisation that is running your workcamp.

££££-£££££ | Interserve

Interserve is an international, interdenominational evangelical Christian fellowship. It organises On Track, a short-term mission programme which aims to encourage cross-cultural Christian service overseas and to provide an opportunity for Christians to experience living, working and sharing their faith in a cross-cultural environment. Typical work may include teaching children, teaching English, working with the handicapped, giving general administrative or secretarial help, caring for children and church work.

HOW LONG IT WILL LAST
Seven to ten months. There are also placements lasting two to three months during the summer.

WHERE YOU CAN GO
Asia, primarily Pakistan and India.

PAYMENT
None.

THE COST TO YOU
You pay for travel to and from and within the country of service, medical, immunisations, insurance and food and accommodation. You also pay £10 application fee, £50 placement fee, and £15 per month after three months.

WHO CAN APPLY
You must be over 18 and a school-leaver or graduate and a committed Christian.

WHEN AND HOW TO APPLY
The closing date for completed application forms is four to five months before the intended date of departure, the main departures being between June and October.

SELECTION PROCESS
In response to enquiry an information leaflet is sent which contains a preliminary application form. When this form is returned a full application form is sent. When this is received and is acceptable, then references are sought. If the references are encouraging, the candidate is called for interview, which determines whether the person is suitable and if a placement can be found.

PLACEMENT
Placements are assessed by the programme staff and offered to participants on the basis of what was discussed at the interview, bearing in mind the applicant's wishes and suitability.

TRAINING
There is a mandatory orientation/training weekend.

SUPPORT FOR PARTICIPANTS
In each country where participants are sent there is a country rep who is responsible for the participant, In addition, each participant has a project supervisor who is responsible for their day-to-day welfare.

££ | Jacob's Well Appeal

This charity runs a long-term project in a Neuropsychiatric Hospital in Siret, Northern Romania, which is 'home' to around 500 children, many of them orphans. The children have mental or physical handicaps or behavioural problems. Many of the children have lacked human stimulation and have not learned to relate to other people. Besides the qualified nurses and other medical staff, there is a need for unqualified volunteers to work with the children and help look after them. There are also two day centres where handicapped children who are still living at home are brought for play and social contact. In addition, volunteers are often able to assist in distributing aid. Volunteers may return to Siret after having had a rest at home for one month. The hours are long and the work and environment hard.

HOW LONG IT WILL LAST
You must be prepared to go for between one and three months.

WHERE YOU CAN GO
Siret, Romania.

PAYMENT
None.

THE COST TO YOU
You will stay as a paying guest with a local family (approximately £15 a week in summer, £18 in winter). You have to pay all your own expenses, including air fare (usually £175 to £225 if you pay student rates), and bring money for personal expenses.

WHO CAN APPLY
You must be at least 18 and in good health, supply good references and pass an interview. Gap year students are welcome.

WHEN AND HOW TO APPLY
Send for introductory information and information about the formal application process. You can apply at any time of year but do so well in advance.

SELECTION PROCESS
One of two coordinators who work alternately in Siret will interview you in depth in England before a decision is made as to your suitability to work in Siret.

PLACEMENT
You will work in the hospital or day centres.

TRAINING
No training is given before you go to Romania, but you will work alongside others to gain the necessary knowledge before being allowed to work with any child on your own.

SUPPORT FOR PARTICIPANTS
You will be told about the work and living conditions in Siret before you go. On arrival you get an induction talk concerning the work, local customs and expected behaviour. While in Siret you have practical and general support from a Romanian coordinator. In the hospital setting you will get advice and support from the hospital coordinator who is a senior member of the hospital staff.

££ | Kibbutz Representatives

This organisation arranges for volunteers to work on a kibbutz. A kibbutz is a co-operative community in Israel, based on agriculture but most now have light industry and many offer tourist facilities. There are over 270 communities, ranging from small communities of 50 people to the largest with over 2000 and an internal bus service. Volunteers work alongside kibbutzniks wherever work is needed for a 48-hour working week (mainly mornings) with three extra days off each month.

HOW LONG IT WILL LAST
The minimum stay is two months (occasionally less in the summer) and the maximum, six months.

WHERE YOU CAN GO
Israel.

PAYMENT
You get accommodation, all meals, leisure facilities, occasional trips and excursions organised by the kibbutz.

THE COST TO YOU
A typical kibbutz package costs about £375, including insurance, and you need £10 for your work visa. You will also need money for travel and insurance, pocket money, and a pre-booking deposit of £60.

WHO CAN APPLY
You must be 18–32, physically and mentally fit, single (or married without children) and have a return ticket or enough money to return home.

WHEN AND HOW TO APPLY
You can apply at any time of the year. Individuals are sent out every day, and at least ten groups per month. But allow three to five weeks for arrangements to be made. Send in your application, then phone after a couple of days to arrange an interview.

SELECTION PROCESS
There is an informal orientation and interview process. This also enables you to decide if working on a kibbutz is really for you.

PLACEMENT
If applicants opt to go with a group, they are sent to a designated kibbutz

for that date which has requested a group in advance. Individual applicants are placed according to vacancies at the time and have a degree of choice.

TRAINING
No training is necessary as kibbutz work for volunteers is usually unskilled. If specific training is needed it will be given at the kibbutz. You do need to be fit for the work.

SUPPORT FOR PARTICIPANTS
There is always back-up on a kibbutz, from arranging the work visa and work-related problems, to those of housing and health (a clinic and nurse are available full-time). The Tel Aviv office can also help with problems and re-allocate volunteers if necessary. The UK office follows up any problems more easily dealt with here.

££££ | Latin Link

Latin Link is a Christian missionary agency working with evangelical churches in Latin America. Its Step Programme enables young people to live and work alongside a Latin American church community helping in a basic building programme. Recent projects have included helping to build orphanages, street kids' shelters, classrooms and community centres in six countries. There are longer-term Stride placements where participants do work tailored to their skills, for example teaching, children's work, church 'planting', Christian publishing, prison visiting and student ministry. Stride volunteers live with a Latin American family and are linked to a support team.

HOW LONG IT WILL LAST
The Step Summer Programme lasts for seven weeks from mid-July, and the Spring Programme runs for four months from mid-March to mid-July. Longer-term Stride placements last from six months to two years.

WHERE YOU CAN GO
Typical placements are Argentina, Bolivia, Brazil, Ecuador and Peru.

PAYMENT
None.

THE COST TO YOU
Latin Link asks for contributions of £1630 towards the Spring Step Programme and £1320 towards Summer Step. This goes towards the cost of your travel, living expenses, a gift to Latin American churches and insurance. You would probably only need to raise approximately a further £370 if you wanted to join a summer team after a spring team. The estimated Stride cost, including flights, administration, orientation, medical insurance and debriefing, is about £1100 plus £275 per month. This excludes pocket money, equipment and immunisations.

WHO CAN APPLY
Step volunteers must be committed Christians between 17 and 35 recommended by their local church. Stride volunteers must be over 18. You don't need to speak Spanish or Portuguese – but it does help, so you are advised to take a basic course before departure. Some disabled people can be placed on Step teams.

WHEN AND HOW TO APPLY
Apply six months before departure to both programmes.

SELECTION PROCESS
Initial selection is based on your application.

PLACEMENT
You will work in a Stride placement or Step team suitable to your skills.

TRAINING
Orientation and training are an integral part of both Step and Stride.

SUPPORT FOR PARTICIPANTS
Applicants are linked to a support team.

£££-£££££ | Oasis

Oasis is a Christian organisation that offers a range of training programmes abroad and in the UK. The programmes are all about learning and doing through a combination of relevant, radical training and hands-on practical placements. Oasis runs two programmes abroad. *Frontline Teams Abroad* (FTA) is a 6-month (or 9-month) project which includes training both in the UK and overseas, learning about a new culture and making a contribution of lasting value. FTA begin in September with a two-week residential training course held in the UK. The team then spends 6 months on placement overseas. The teams in France and Germany spend 9 months overseas. *Frontline Global Links* (FGL) is a six-week life-changing experience for those wanting to spend their summer doing something really worthwhile. Ideal if you want to find out if overseas work is for you.

Oasis also provides programmes in the UK. *Frontline Teams UK* offers you 10 months of hands-on experience working alongside a local church, combined with a programme of training. Other opportunities with Oasis include the Oasis Youth Ministry Course, Frontline Urban Exposure and Frontline Impact Teams.

HOW LONG IT WILL LAST
FTA lasts six or nine months and FGL lasts six weeks.

WHERE YOU CAN GO
Frontline Teams Abroad go to Peru, Brazil, France, Germany, Portugal, Romania, Zimbabwe, Kenya and Uganda. As a member of a Frontline Team UK you will work in an urban inner-city church.

PAYMENT
None.

THE COST TO YOU
The total cost of Frontline Teams Abroad is £2990. This cost covers training in the UK and abroad, travel to and from the country, insurance, work travel, food, accommodation, administration, costs and a holiday allowance. For Frontline Teams UK you need to raise £2200. The exact fee will be confirmed on your selection day.

WHO CAN APPLY
Christians between 18 and 30.

WHEN AND HOW TO APPLY
Enquiries by post, fax or E-mail to the Oasis office. You will be sent further information, including an application form. The closing date for Frontline Teams Abroad is June and for Frontline Teams UK July.

SELECTION PROCESS
All participants attend a selection weekend where they find out more about the projects and are interviewed by members of staff. Places are offered as a result of this.

PLACEMENT
Placements are allocated by Oasis staff as a result of the selection weekends, although some preferences from participants may be taken into account.

TRAINING
Frontline Teams Abroad are given two weeks of orientation training prior to your departure, as well as weekly training sessions during your time in your chosen location. Frontline Teams UK have a weekly training session which provides an in-depth, radical look at Christianity and today's world.

SUPPORT FOR PARTICIPANTS
You will be sent out in teams which vary in size, and a team leader is responsible for each team. You are looked after by your church placements and coordinators who are employed by Oasis Trust to oversee your wellbeing.

£££££ | Operation Mobilisation

This is an evangelical Christian training organisation which sends volunteers overseas. Teams are both interdenominational and international. There are short- and long-term possibilities providing opportunities for direct evangelistic outreach, support services or specific professional roles. The Global Action programme is the one that will probably interest gap year students most.

HOW LONG IT WILL LAST
Global Action lasts for one or two years. There are also short-term opportunities available.

WHERE YOU CAN GO
Operation Mobilisation works in over 80 different countries.

PAYMENT
None.

THE COST TO YOU
This depends on how long you go for and what country you visit, but could be anything from £300 to £600 per month. In addition, the orientation conference and travel to it will cost about £300. There is a £25 registration fee.

WHO CAN APPLY
You should be between 17 and 70 and have the support of your home church. To join a one-year training programme you should normally first take part in a short-term campaign.

WHEN AND HOW TO APPLY
There are two intakes for new recruits – at the beginning of January and end of August. Everyone who wants to participate should first take part in a short-term outreach, such as Easter Evangelism or Summer Challenge. Write to the OM office for a Global Action options pack and application form. You will need to supply two references and a medical report.

SELECTION PROCESS
You visit the Quinta office for an interview and then attend an international recruiting conference.

PLACEMENT
You can discuss this with OM.

TRAINING
Operation Mobilisation includes a Bible Study programme and conferences and seminars.

SUPPORT FOR PARTICIPANTS
Volunteers are supported by OM and their home church.

£££££

SAMS (South American Mission Society)

This is an Anglican mission society which can offer places on short-term team projects or individual placements. Examples of individual placements include living with a mission partner/family and helping with family life; working in a local church with outreach programmes; helping young people with English conversation; voluntary teaching; working in a church-sponsored orphanage or with a programme for street children.

HOW LONG IT WILL LAST
Individual placements last from a minimum of six months up to a year. Team projects last a few weeks.

WHERE YOU CAN GO
South America, Spain and Portugal.

PAYMENT
None.

THE COST TO YOU
Short-term teams cost from £250 to £1000. Basic costs for individual placements are £1160–£1660, which includes administration, an orientation course, documentation and innoculations, return airfare and travel and medical insurance. You will also need living costs of about £350 per month.

WHO CAN APPLY
You must be a committed Christian willing to work directly with, and under the supervision of, the National Anglican Church. A basic knowledge of Spanish is useful.

WHEN AND HOW TO APPLY
Write to SAMS for information and an application form.

SELECTION PROCESS
There is a Selection process involving an interview.

PLACEMENT
The initial suggestion for a placement comes from SAMS, although you can decline it.

TRAINING
You are advised to read widely about the country you are going to, and to learn the language.

SUPPORT FOR PARTICIPANTS
On short-term teams a member of the team will be directly responsible for you. On individual placements you will receive support from the local church, including a supervisor for personal support who will be your first port of call if you have any problems.

£££ Staffansgården

This is a Camphill community for handicapped children (see chapter 5). It has five households, and volunteers help with household chores and care of the residents. During the week all co-workers and residents work in a workshop or house. The main workshops consists of woodwork, weaving, baking, farm, vegetable garden and candle making. You work six days a week.

HOW LONG IT WILL LAST
The minimum stay is six months but a year's stay is preferred.

WHERE YOU CAN GO
300km north of Stockholm, Sweden.

PAYMENT
Free board and lodging, monthly pocket money and holiday money according to your length of stay.

THE COST TO YOU
You have to find your own travel expenses to the Community.

WHO CAN APPLY
You must be 19 or over and not a drug-taker. As the Community receives many applications, people who can stay for at least a year are given preference, especially those with a knowledge of Swedish. However, volunteers who do not speak Swedish are not excluded but are expected to take part in the community's Swedish classes.

WHEN AND HOW TO APPLY
Apply to Staffansgården and include your personal details, CV, testimonials and references, and photo; say when and for how long you want to stay; why you want to go; any special wishes or needs; how you found out about Staffansgården; and whether you have a driving licence.

SELECTION PROCESS
Selection is at the discretion of Staffansgården.

PLACEMENT
You will work at Staffansgården.

TRAINING
You will be introduced to the background of the teaching ideologies by taking part in a seminar once a week which includes artistic activities.

SUPPORT FOR PARTICIPANTS
You will be supported within the Community.

££££

The Sunseed Trust

This charity tries to improve the quality of life and environment of people living in and near desert areas of the world. You help on the projects and with the day-to-day running of the group. The projects include finding and spreading new ways of fuel use, plant growing, water provision and conservation, recycling of nutrients, effective treatment and use of human and vegetable wastes and labour and energy-saving methods. The Sunseed Trust operates a centre in Spain and also runs a research programme in Tanzania.

HOW LONG IT WILL LAST
Full-time volunteers (FTVs) join for five weeks or more.

WHERE YOU CAN GO
Spain.

PAYMENT
None.

THE COST TO YOU
The costs (2000) in Spain are £54 per week for the first five weeks (FTV) in low season and £60 per week in high season. After five weeks you pay less. If you only stay for one week you pay £20 extra. These prices entitle you to full board and travel insurance. Travel to Spain costs about £90. There is a registration fee of £55.

WHO CAN APPLY
Anyone over 16 can apply, but 16 or 17 year olds must have their guardian's consent and a reference about their maturity.

WHEN AND HOW TO APPLY
For a five-week stay as a FTV (e.g. as a student placement) phone to check if space is available and send £5 for a full information pack. Then send a completed registration form, registration fee, CV, address and phone number, and medical history directly to Spain. You can expect to hear in two to three weeks. Try to give at least three weeks' notice.

SELECTION PROCESS
There is no Selection process for working visitors. FTVs who are specialists in either botany or appropriate technology may agree their programme of work in advance with the relevant head of department. General volunteers usually agree their programme on arrival after the first week. Volunteers are accepted if space is available.

TRAINING
Supervision is given by the head of department in the relevant field.

SUPPORT FOR PARTICIPANTS
Sunseed run a kindly, supportive residential centre. Staff, FTVs and working visitors share routine jobs. FTVs are expected to take some special responsibility and may lead working visitors.

££–££££ | Teaching & Projects Abroad

Teaching & Projects Abroad aims to help others learn English. The programmes offer volunteers who want to travel and teach a chance to do so in an interesting part of the world. You work about 18 hours a week teaching English. The type of teaching varies from place to place, but usually classes might consist of schoolchildren or adults. You are housed with local families or other teachers in comfortable hostels. Teaching & Projects Abroad also organises business/professional work experience.

HOW LONG IT WILL LAST
The programmes last from one month or more.

WHERE YOU CAN GO
India, Ghana, Russia, Ukraine, Brazil, China, Mexico, Nepal, Tibet, Togo or Zimbabwe.

PAYMENT
There is no payment.

THE COST TO YOU
The cost varies from £945 upwards, including travel. You will also need pocket money.

WHO CAN APPLY
Students 17+ after A-levels/Highers and entering university. Non-UK passport holders with good spoken English are welcome.

WHEN AND HOW TO APPLY
You can join Teaching & Projects Abroad at any time of the year. There is an application form at the back of the Teaching & Projects Abroad brochure.

SELECTION
There is no Selection process, although you can attend optional interviews and Open Days.

PLACEMENT
Once your application form and deposit have been received, Teaching & Projects Abroad will try to book you on the programme you want. If you can't be booked on the programme you have chosen, another programme will be suggested or your deposit returned in full.

TRAINING
Teaching & Projects Abroad will supply you with lots of ideas for devising your own teaching programme. There is an optional TEFL foundation course and local language and culture courses at your destination.

SUPPORT FOR PARTICIPANTS
Teaching & Projects Abroad have permanent staff in each placement. The fee includes first-class medical and travel insurance.

££££ | Tearfund

This is an evangelical Christian organisation which offers several kinds of short-term voluntary placements overseas, plus a number of opportunities in the UK. As a Transform International member, you take part in practical work such as building or making water tanks, or using skills with people such as underprivileged children, or on youth camps. You will also have the opportunity to see and reflect – through discussions and visits to other projects – on issues such as poverty. Transform UK teams work with people

113

in inner-city areas. Transform teams work with Tearfund partners within the country, i.e. the local church or church-based people.

HOW LONG IT WILL LAST

Transform International teams last from for four to six weeks during July to September. Occasionally there are teams at other times. For UK urban work, Tearfund runs two-week or one-year programmes called Transform UK and Transform 365 respectively. The former happens during the summer.

WHERE YOU CAN GO

Africa, Europe, Middle East, Latin America or the Caribbean, or urban areas of the UK (e.g. Glasgow, Belfast, London or Manchester).

PAYMENT

None.

THE COST TO YOU

To take part in a six-week Transform team costs about £1300. Costs for some teams can increase or reduce by approximately £50 depending on length or location. You will need spending money, the cost of any pre-departure medicals/vaccinations and the cost of travel to the orientation course and reunion weekend. The two-week urban teams cost £95.

WHO CAN APPLY

You must be an evangelical Christian aged 17+ for UK teams and 18 or over for overseas service.

WHEN AND HOW TO APPLY

Write to Transform Programme at Tearfund for an application form. You will also be sent reference forms for a work supervisor and your church leader. The closing date for international teams is 1 March. For UK teams it is 31 May.

SELECTION PROCESS

You attend a selection day for Transform International. This may be held at a regional site or at Teddington, Middlesex, about four months before departure date.

PLACEMENT

Venues are confirmed after selection, at the discretion of Tearfund.

TRAINING

You attend a residential orientation course and a reunion weekend.

SUPPORT FOR PARTICIPANTS

Teams are led by people who are known to Tearfund and who have had previous leadership and overseas experience. All practical arrangements, including flights and insurance, are made by Tearfund and the organis-ation provides a comprehensive information pack which includes advice on things such as vaccinations and anti-malaria protection.

£££-£££££

World Exchange, Scottish Churches

World Exchange is a programme of a group of Scottish and British churches which sends people to work abroad. Placements are with community organisations and projects are linked to partner churches.

HOW LONG IT WILL LAST
Placements usually last 12 months.

WHERE YOU CAN GO
Lebanon, Hungary, Romania, Guatemala, Malawi, South Africa, India, Pakistan and Thailand.

PAYMENT
You are provided with accommodation and a living allowance to cover food and pocket money.

THE COST TO YOU
You will have to raise money towards the cost of your placement which will contribute to the air fare, insurance and training.

WHO CAN APPLY
World Exchange can consider people with a wide range of experience, of any age from school-leavers onwards.

WHEN AND HOW TO APPLY
Enquiries are welcome at any time. Contact World Exchange for more information.

SELECTION PROCESS
Selection is at the discretion of World Exchange.

PLACEMENT
The placement is arranged by World Exchange.

TRAINING
World Exchange provides a basic training programme.

SUPPORT FOR PARTICIPANTS
You are given support by World Exchange both overseas and on your return.

£££-£££££

World Horizons

This is a world-wide prayer-based mission movement that has some part-time volunteers.

HOW LONG IT WILL LAST
Volunteers participate for a year at a time.

WHERE YOU CAN GO
World Horizons has people working in 31 countries.

PAYMENT
None.

THE COST TO YOU
You will have to find all your fares and living expenses.

WHO CAN APPLY
Anyone who is a committed Christian.

WHEN AND HOW TO APPLY
Apply by letter at any time, stating the country and field of work you are interested in, the length of time available, etc. Any personal details are helpful.

SELECTION PROCESS
Selection is made on the basis of the application forms, references, interview and liaison with the overseas team involved.

PLACEMENT
World Horizons does not look for people to fill any specific vacancies but decides with the individual volunteer they best way forward for them.

TRAINING
You learn on-the-job.

SUPPORT FOR PARTICIPANTS
Support comes from within the team.

£+

Youth Action for Peace UK (YAP)

This is a Christian organisation which arranges international youth exchanges. YAP sends volunteers to work abroad in groups on short-term work camps lasting a few weeks, although longer-term projects lasting several months are possible. The aim of the longer-term projects is to integrate a volunteer into a local community project and give him/her the opportunity to learn a new language and to discover a region. In exchange, the volunteer will help the project in its management and in organising local action. There are also projects in Britain.

HOW LONG IT WILL LAST
Most projects last one to four weeks, during June to September. The longer placements can last from three months to a year.

WHERE YOU CAN GO
Europe, the Middle East, India, North Africa Latin America.

PAYMENT
Food and accommodation are provided. For longer-term projects only, pocket money is provided as well as some travel reimbursement.

THE COST TO YOU
A small registration fee for work camps plus membership of British YAP.

WHO CAN APPLY
You must be aged 18 or over for work camps and 18–25 for longer projects. You do not usually need a knowledge of the language of the host country (unless specified).

WHEN AND HOW TO APPLY
Write to YAP specifying whether you are interested in work camps or long-term projects. A brochure with a complete list of short-term projects is published in April. Applications are on a first come, first served basis. Send a completed application form plus cheque for the total fees. On acceptance you receive details, travel directions and insurance form. Selection for long-term projects takes place in May/June.

SELECTION PROCESS
Selection is at the discretion of YAP.

PLACEMENT TRAINING
There is a briefing meeting designed to give an insight into the cultural and social characteristics of Eastern European and Islamic countries for volunteers to eastern/central Europe, North Africa and the Middle East. Attendance is recommended.

SUPPORT FOR PARTICIPANTS
A local person is appointed to run the project.

£££££ | Year for God

Youth with a Mission is an international evangelical movement of Christians from many denominations. It runs a Year For God programme, starting in September, which offers an opportunity to be part of a YWAM relief-development project in a developing country. Projects range from caring for street children and teaching them to read, to practical activities such as drilling boreholes and repairing houses.

HOW LONG IT WILL LAST
One year.

WHERE YOU CAN GO
Recently teams have been to Argentina, Russia and Uganda.

PAYMENT
None.

THE COST TO YOU

You will need to raise your own money – between £3500 and £4000, depending on location. This includes air fare, food and accommodation, Discipleship Training School, medical insurance, orientation and debriefing. You will also need some personal spending money.

WHO CAN APPLY

Mature 18 year olds will be considered, although the usual age is 21. You do not need a second language as all lectures, etc, are translated into English, but you are encouraged to learn the local language throughout the year.

WHEN AND HOW TO APPLY

Every applicant is asked to attend an Enquiry Weekend (details and application forms available from the Year Teams office). You will later need to complete a full application form and provide references from your church leader, tutor or employer and doctor. Ask for these when you apply for an Enquiry Weekend form. It is helpful but not essential to complete them before the Enquiry Weekend.

SELECTION PROCESS

You will be given a personal interview.

PLACEMENT

Your suitability for your chosen course will be discussed at your interview.

TRAINING

Five-day orientation in England before teams are sent out. You will complete a Discipleship Training School in the field, which comprises three months of lectures and two to three months of outreach.

SUPPORT FOR PARTICIPANTS

You will work under the guidance of experienced leaders.

Travel and
holidays
in the UK

TRAVEL AND HOLIDAYS IN THE UK

Not everyone wants to work during their gap year, or necessarily to go abroad. There are many ways of extending your horizons and experiences without leaving the UK. Both travel and holidays come under this heading.

Of course, many people consider things such as environmental projects to be holidays – it all depends what your interests are and what you regard as work or pleasure. So some of the ideas mentioned in this chapter may overlap with other chapters.

Your holiday is likely to take up only part of your year out in any case. It might be for a week or two before you start a gap year job, as a break between year-out options, or to relax at the end of your year out before going to college. Some of the ideas in this section are therefore of a few weeks duration.

Many pursuits in the UK are organised so that you get the most out of the experience. These have the advantage of being vetted for safety in advance and have experienced people running them. Working holidays are another option. People from towns used to go hop picking as their summer holiday treat. There is no reason why you should not do something similar.

UK holidays are often, though not necessarily, cheaper than those abroad. Even more so if you stay at home and your parents are willing to give you board and lodging. But you should consider leaving home for at least part of the time if you want a new experience. If you do stay at home you should think how you can contribute to the family finances – it does cost parents money to keep you and at your age you should be expecting to pay your way.

If you are travelling to several places throughout the UK, particularly if you are taking a walking or cycling holiday, consider joining the Youth Hostels Association (YHA) for reasonably priced accommodation and food. The Ramblers Association and the Cyclists Touring Club are useful contacts too. Out of season, bed and breakfast places may be worthwhile trying – ask at the local tourist information office. Look on college notice boards for information about shared accommodation if you intend to stay in one place for any length of time.

There are many kinds of holidays that offer interesting experiences but which are not too expensive. College-based holidays, where you can take part in an activity, are good value for money but do not last more than a few weeks. Ask in your local library for information about universities and colleges that host holiday activities. Some holiday and travel ideas are given below.

Camping is a cheap way of taking a holiday, but groups of young men should be aware that some campsites will not accept them because they are concerned about noise and disruption (however unfair that may be to individuals). You may need to book in advance for campsites, especially in high season. But some places – Ireland, for example – have a more flexible approach to camping and you may be able to camp in a farmer's field after asking permission.

Travel in the UK

You can travel cheaply on trains all over the UK by applying for a Young Person's Railcard at a mainline railway station. This is for anyone aged between 16 and 26. You need two passport photos and proof of age such as a birth certificate or proof of student status from your school or college. Use the Railcard to get a third off all your leisure fares throughout the UK. For local areas, buy bus or rail rover tickets which allow you to travel for a number of days in a particular area for a cheaper-than-normal price. Contact National Rail Enquiries, National Express or London Transport for information about their services.

Coaches are another cheap and easy of travelling long distances, but you should allow for the fact that they may take longer than trains. Modern coaches have toilets and comfortable seats. Book in advance if possible.

Do not hitch-hike. Reports about the deaths and abductions of hitch-hikers should be enough to put anyone off. In many European countries hitch-hiking is now illegal.

Friends

Going on holiday or travelling with friends in the UK can make the time more enjoyable. But bear in mind that if you are going away for a long time you should be able to get on well together. The advantage of travelling together in the UK is that if you do fall out there is not so far to get home! Also some places (such as campsites as mentioned above) dislike groups of young men. Getting accommodation could be difficult for groups.

Safeguards

Your safety must be paramount. Don't assume that because you are in another part of the country that your usual safety precautions do not apply.

Do not walk alone in the dark in back streets or alleyways, stick to main streets. If you are followed, run to the nearest lighted place – a shop, pub or house and call for help. Women should carry a rape alarm. You can get attacked wherever you are. Do not travel in an empty train compartment. If someone who lives locally tells you that a particular part of their town is unsafe, then it probably is. Most places have their 'black' spots.

Women-only holidays

Having fought long and hard for equality, it may seem strange that women might prefer a single-sex holiday. But some women do like to take time out to relax in an all-female atmosphere. Some organisations which run general schemes do organise women-only programmes, for example on sailing or adventure courses.

You can, of course, combine travel with other pursuits such as sport, a hobby, or work. The latter might be a good way of funding your travel and leisure time. It can also be fun in its own right (see previous chapters).

£

BTCV (British Trust for Conservation Volunteers)

This is the country's largest practical conservation charity and can provide a wide range of opportunities to help protect and improve the environment. These include over 500 conservation working holidays each year in the UK and overseas, conservation volunteering opportunities, involvement in local community groups and training opportunities.

Working holidays last from three to ten days and include projects such as wetland management in the Norfolk Broads, tree planting in the Scottish Highlands, dry stone walling in Cumbria or turtle protection on the Island of Rhodes. Prices start at £23 for a weekend and £45 for a week to cover food, accommodation and training skills. No experience is necessary.

There are also opportunities for volunteers to help BTCV. You could be a Volunteer Officer (VO) for three months or more based at a BTCV office, be a Support Volunteer working at a BTCV office on a regular basis, perhaps once or twice a week, or join one of BTCV's midweek or weekend groups getting hands-on training in conservation techniques once a week. Volunteers are given comprehensive training and there are opportunities to manage projects or gain nationally recognised qualifications such as NVQs. For details of the opportunities available, contact BTCV.

£

Cathedral Camps

Going on a Cathedral Camp is an unusual way of spending a holiday, but it also gives you the chance to visit some of Great Britain's finest cities. Volunteers help with conservation and restoration at Cathedrals and their environments. Much of the work is 'routine maintenance' but is interesting, varied and constructive. Although the camps only last a week, many people like to go on several of them. Work at a camp can be entered for part of the Duke of Edinburgh's Award Scheme.

HOW LONG IT WILL LAST
Camps last for one week each.

WHERE YOU CAN GO
Cathedral cities all over Britain.

PAYMENT
None.

THE COST TO YOU
It costs £50 per camp to take part.

WHO CAN APPLY
You must be over 16 and under 30. You do not have to be a member of any religious denomination. Disabled people are welcome.

WHEN AND HOW TO APPLY
Contact Cathedral Camps for an application form and return it with payment and a large stamped addressed envelope.

SELECTION
There is no selection process.

PLACEMENT
You apply for the camp or camps you want to attend.

TRAINING
Instruction is given by experts.

SUPPORT FOR PARTICIPANTS
All jobs are supervised by cathedral staff. A leader is responsible for running your camp.

£-££

CBA (Council For British Archaeology)

For a holiday that will take you out of doors and at the same time help to discover the UK's heritage, why not take part in an archaeological project. This usually involves fieldwork based on excavations (commonly known as 'digs'). The CBA does not organise fieldwork itself, but acts as an information service about fieldwork in the United Kingdom. The information is circulated in a supplement, *CBA Briefing*, that appears in every other issue of the CBA's magazine *British Archaeology*, and is also published on the Internet. *Briefing* occasionally includes information about a few overseas projects (but see Archaeology Abroad, in chapter 8). Conditions on each project vary so it is important to contact the organisation running the fieldwork for details.

HOW LONG IT WILL LAST
The duration of projects varies, but most take place for a month or more during the summer season. Organisers usually ask volunteers to stay for at least a week; some stipulate a minimum stay of two weeks. You can, of course, stay longer and some people like to stay for the whole season.

WHERE YOU CAN GO
There are opportunities throughout the United Kingdom.

PAYMENT
Usually none, unless you have some experience and expertise.

THE COST TO YOU
Membership of the CBA costs £24 a year, with a reduced rate for full-time students. The cost of taking part in fieldwork varies. Some projects will provide free basic accommodation such as campsite, washing facilities and perhaps a meal. Others might charge a subsistence fee of about £80 for use of basic facilities and meals. Training digs where instruction is given in archaeological techniques and theory can cost £100 a week or more.

WHO CAN APPLY
The level of expertise and age required varies, so contact the organisers for details. Some excavations particularly welcome beginners.

WHEN AND HOW TO APPLY.
Contact the organiser of your preferred project directly at the address given in *Briefing*.

SELECTION
There is usually no formal procedure but selection is at the discretion of the site director. In some cases this might depend on your experience and expertise.

PLACEMENT
You choose the excavation you want to work on and apply accordingly.

TRAINING
Training excavations have a programme of instruction in technique and theory, but most projects suitable for beginners provide basic training on-the-job .

SUPPORT FOR PARTICIPANTS
The site will have a director and site supervisor as well as assistants.

£–££
The National Trust

The National Trust organises working holidays throughout Britain. Although these are usually short-term holidays, they can be combined with other things or you could do several in different parts of the country. The holidays are not only fun but at the same time make a valuable contribution to the conservation of the landscape. Most of the holidays involve conservation tasks such as drystone walling or woodland footpath construction. Others are more specialised and involve botanical surveys, building construction or archaeology, for example.

You normally stay in a NT base camp such as a converted farmhouse, stable block or cottage. The day runs from 9 to 5, with breaks, and everyone takes a turn with domestic chores and cooking. You will have evenings and a half-day a week off. Experienced volunteers or people with a relevant background can volunteer to help run a working holiday and are given relevant training.

HOW LONG IT WILL LAST
They last about a week on average.

WHERE YOU CAN GO
England, Wales and Northern Ireland.

PAYMENT
None.

THE COST TO YOU
Approximately £20 to £150, depending on the length and type of project.

WHO CAN APPLY
The holidays have different minimum ages; some take you from 16, others 18, others 21.

WHEN AND HOW TO APPLY
Send for a brochure listing the holidays. Holidays take place throughout the year.

TRAINING
Training is given on-the-job.

SUPPORT FOR PARTICIPANTS
Every project has a trained leader and NT Warden.

££

Ocean Youth Trust

The Ocean Youth Trust offers over 300 voyages each year. It provides adventurous sailing opportunities on its fleet of modern 70-foot vessels. OYT takes part in Tall Ships races. On most vessels there is room for twelve participants.

HOW LONG IT WILL LAST
Voyages are weekend, midweek or week-long. The yachts sail from March to November each year.

WHERE YOU CAN GO
The vessels operate from ports on Great Britain and Northern Ireland, and European ports are frequently visited.

PAYMENT
None.

THE COST TO YOU
Prices vary between low and high season and the length of voyage – from £110 to £441. If you can't afford the voyage fees yourself, OYT may be able to help you through its grant scheme and local fundraising groups.

WHO CAN APPLY
You must be aged 12–24 and able to swim. No previous sailing experience is required.

WHEN AND HOW TO APPLY
Contact OYT for a brochure and provisional booking form. Select your voyage from the programme then phone your local office to book, or return the reply slip.

SELECTION
There is no Selection process.

PLACEMENT
You apply for the voyage you want and will be placed on it if there is room.

TRAINING
You are taught the necessary skills during the voyage and can gain RYA Competent Crew and Watch Leader certificates on many OYT voyages. You can also complete your Duke of Edinburgh's Award: Gold Residential.

SUPPORT FOR PARTICIPANTS
OYT provides all the safety equipment and wet weather gear necessary for sailing. Each vessel operates under a fully qualified skipper and a team of qualified leaders. OYT operates a safety reporting system, with vessels reporting every 24 hours, backed up by a 24-hour shore contact system.

£ | Sustrans

If you like cycling and want a cheap and enjoyable holiday, you can enjoy many miles of safe cycling through beautiful parts of Britain thanks to Sustrans and the National Cycle Network. Sustrans, a practical civil engineering charity, is coordinating the creation of the National Cycle Network. The National Cycle Network is a millennium project to create 6500 miles of safe, high quality and signposted routes for cyclists by the year 2005. Some routes are already in use and others are being created. You can support the Network by joining Sustrans, which also sells maps of the routes and other helpful literature.

Supporters of Sustrans also have the chance to join in many different events every year from May to September. Perhaps the most interesting to gap year students are the workcamps organised each year so that members can help to build the National Cycle Network. Participants help with construction tasks such as fencing, draining and clearing vegetation.

HOW LONG IT WILL LAST
Workcamps last for two weeks and at the time of writing there are six a year, although they will increase in number and size as the millennium approaches. Sustrans prefers a minimum of three days' involvement but some people like to take part in several or all of the camps.

WHERE YOU CAN GO
Workcamps take place at British locations where the network needs building.

PAYMENT
None.

THE COST TO YOU
Supporting Sustrans costs a minimum £15 per year. At the time of writing the concessionary student rate for attending a camp is £5 per day or £15 for one camp (two weeks). You can go on more than one camp and this is good value. If you went on six camps, for example, it would cost you £40. These prices may increase. Cooking facilities are provided, but you are responsible for your own food and accommodation. Sustrans will provide an accommodation list with details of indoor and camping options nearby. They will also try to arrange other cheap options such as a farmer's field or village hall.

WHO CAN APPLY
Camps are open to supporters of Sustrans. There is a maximum of 40–50 residential workers at each camp.

WHEN AND HOW TO APPLY
Contact Sustrans for details of membership and events.

TRAINING
Each morning there is a use-of-tools and health and safety training session. The site engineer briefs participants each morning on the day's tasks.

SUPPORT FOR PARTICIPANTS
Qualified first-aiders and medical kits are available on site. The practical construction works at each site is organised and run by a core construction team and project engineer. A 'household' manager organises accommodation, food and entertainment with assistance from volunteers.

£

Waterways Recovery Group (WRG)

If you want to spend some time in the open air doing something constructive, you might be interested in the Waterways Recovery Group. WRG is part of the Inland Waterways Association and it arranges restoration and recovery work on waterways and canals in Britain. The work can involve anything from basic clearance and digging to more complicated reconstruction work. The WRG's Canal Camps are an enjoyable way to find out about canal restoration as part of a team. Most people go on their own and have a good time. You are welcome to go with one friend: large groups of friends tend to upset the team spirit of the camps. You can take part of your Duke of Edinburgh's Award at a camp.

HOW LONG IT WILL LAST
Canal Camps last for a week at a time throughout most of the year. Regional groups also work at weekends on sites around the country.

WHERE YOU CAN GO
There are sites throughout Britain.

PAYMENT
None.

THE COST TO YOU
Canal Camp weeks cost £35, including accommodation in village or school halls and food. You will need to find the cost of transport to the site too.

WHO CAN APPLY
Anyone aged over 17 and under 70 can apply. No special skills are required, but you need to be reasonably fit.

WHEN AND HOW TO APPLY
Write to WRG at the beginning of the year (January/February) for their Canal Camps brochure.

SELECTION
There is no Selection process.

PLACEMENT
You choose the camp you want to go on. The only restrictions are due to the number of places available at each camp.

TRAINING
Any training required is provided.

SUPPORT FOR PARTICIPANTS
All participants are covered by insurance. Each camp has a camp leader and other experienced people to support you.

WWOOF (Willing Workers on Organic Farms)

WWOOF puts people in touch with organic farmers, gardeners and smallholders who want the help. You are expected to work an average of six hours a day for your keep and the opportunity to learn about organic growing. The work varies from farm to farm, but is suitable for most applicants. Some farms particularly welcome beginners. Occasionally farmers express a preference for people with specific skills such a drystone walling. There are also opportunities for WWOOF work overseas.

HOW LONG IT WILL LAST

Stays are normally weekend or midweek, but longer stays are often possible, particularly in Scotland. Some overseas farms can offer work for a month or much longer.

WHERE YOU CAN GO

There is work available throughout England, Scotland and Wales and overseas through WWOOF International.

PAYMENT

You will get meals and accommodation, the opportunity to learn and, if necessary, transport to and from the local station.

THE COST TO YOU

You will need to pay membership of WWOOF, and for the cost of travel to and from the farms. You will also need you own sleeping bag, weatherproof clothing, work gloves and boots.

WHO CAN APPLY

Everyone of 16 and over is welcome.

WHEN AND HOW TO APPLY

Send a stamped, addressed envelope to WWOOF for a brochure and application form. Once you have joined you get regular lists of farms and dates where help is needed, and you apply for them through WWOOF. Once you have completed at least four days of WWOOF-type work you are sent details of places you can contact direct. You can apply directly to Scottish farms immediately, and because of the distance involved stays of longer than a weekend are usual there.

SELECTION

There is no selection process.

PLACEMENT

You go to the farm you have booked for if there are places available.

TRAINING

You will be given instructions by your host.

SUPPORT FOR PARTICIPANTS

WWOOF is run by a Coordinator and a team of voluntary helpers. If you have a complaint you can let the WWOOF Ombudsman or Regional Organiser know.

8

TRAVEL AND HOLIDAYS ABROAD

One of the safest and best ways to travel abroad is with an organised holiday group. This can either be with a travel or exploration group or with a tour operator. These holidays are sometimes cheaper than individually arranged holidays, because of bulk discounting. Holidays abroad are as varied as your imagination. They could be for leisure only, guided tours or working holidays. You might also regard some of the overseas activities described in other chapters in this book as holidays – kibbutz or conservation work, for example.

If you travel with an organisation, the costs are usually all-inclusive so all you will pay for is spending money. If you arrange your own holiday or travel, you will have to find travel costs, accommodation, food, visa, passport, medical fees, etc. This can add up to more than you anticipated. You can cut costs by staying in college accommodation or digs out of the centre of towns. Buy a student or young person's travel pass for the country you are visiting. Get an international student card if you are eligible, to get you into museums and art galleries cheaper. Take money in the form of travellers cheques or a credit card, if possible. Do not carry more than a little money in foreign currency.

Safeguards

Your safety is just as important abroad as at home. Do not assume that you are safer abroad. Take the usual precautions of not going off with strangers or walking alone in unlit or unpopulated places after dark. Do not wear expensive jewellery, and carry your money and passport in a money bag around your waist or neck. Women should not wear revealing clothing unless on a beach in a large tourist resort. If you are sexually harassed or assaulted, tell the tour rep and the police immediately. Respect the religious laws and customs of whatever country you are in.

Do not assume that sexual behaviour is the same everywhere. Many countries have much stricter rules about such matters. Young men in particular could have their intentions misconstrued. If you have sex abroad always use a condom. Holiday romances can be fun but do not take them too seriously – they usually do not survive the return home.

Travelling with friends

It can be more fun to take a holiday with friends, but make sure you get on well. If you think the behaviour of the group is going to be unacceptable to you, decline to go – there is no point in getting into trouble because of someone else's boorish behaviour. If you intend spending a long time with a particular group of friends, try to spend a short holiday with them first to see if you all get on well together. If not, change your mind about spending a longer time with them. If you do travel on your own it may be cheaper and quicker, but you must be more aware of your safety.

Arranging your own holiday

Many countries sell travel passes and long-term tickets to enable young people to travel around the country. These are worth buying, but you need to have saved up the cost beforehand. Arrange any visas well in advance and check that your passport will be valid for the whole time you are abroad, and six months longer for some countries. Book tickets through a reputable travel agent.

When using European trains, try to book a seat in advance. Most people book seats and if you don't you run the risk of having to stand throughout the whole journey.

Ask where to buy local tickets for buses when abroad. You often need to buy one before boarding, perhaps from newsagents, kiosks or street vendors. In Italy, for example, you must buy your bus ticket from a kiosk before boarding.

When arriving in a strange town do not take the hotel nearest the station – it may be cheap but it may also be the local brothel. Either get advice from a travel agent before you go or ask the tourist information office when you get there. Try to pre-book if possible. Do not accept lodgings from strangers, however friendly they seem.

Travel companies

Arranging a holiday through a standard tour operator can be cheap because of the block bookings they make. They can often find you a cheap holiday, especially if you are flexible about the places and times you can travel. You are even more likely to be able to travel cheaply if you are prepared to accept a booking at very short notice. If you are booking a self-catering or hotel holiday, you (or one of your party) must be 18 to sign the agreement.

Travel agencies, specially small ones, often advertise cheap holidays in their windows; many others advertise in the small ads of the newspapers.

So called 'bucket shops' which sell holidays very cheap to fill up spaces on planes or packages often have very good deals for the flexible traveller, but check that they are members of ABTA. To take advantage of cheap deals you will need to have all your visas, injections and passport up to date so that you can leave at short notice.

Organisations which specialise in catering for students can help you plan an itinerary and sort out 'open' tickets or rover tickets. Many European countries have rover-type tickets.

Good travel companies can help you plan an itinerary and advise on and/or arrange accommodation, plane and train travel and give advice about countries' entry requirements – all within your budget. Some companies specialise in advising on and arranging holidays for the independent traveller.

There are several travel agencies that cater especially for students and can give gap year students help with planning their trips and arranging cheap flights, coach, rail and specialised tickets. Contact them for specific advice about the trip you want to make. The ones described in the section below are only examples. A selection of other travel companies that offer exciting holidays is also included. There are many more – check the small ads in the Sunday papers and magazines such as *Private Eye*.

Wherever you go, make sure that you take at least one good map and guide book with you. You will usually be able to buy local versions after you arrive, but don't bank on it. It is better to start out with basic instructions in a language you can understand.

The organisations listed below offer ideas for holidays and include some specialist travel companies.

£-£££ Archaeology Abroad

If you want an overseas holiday with a difference, why not try taking part in an excavation abroad? If you like history and hard work, this could be the ideal holiday for you. Archaeology Abroad provides information about opportunities for archaeological fieldwork and excavation outside the UK. Bulletins are published in March, May and October each year and advertise about 500–800 places for volunteers and staff in about fifteen countries. Although Archaeology Abroad cannot inspect the sites, it tries to publish information only from reputable, professional archaeologists and institutions.

The March Bulletin contains information on excavations taking place in the summer and autumn of that year, the May bulletin contains additional information received since March with details of digs still available, and the October bulletin tells you about excavations early the following year, with updated information about the British Schools and Institutes and their grants and scholarships. All issues carry comprehensive notes and guidance and information about the activities of related organisations, publications and study courses, etc.

Opportunities for fieldwork overseas vary considerably around the world. Archaeology Abroad issues fact sheets for volunteers about countries from which few advertisements are received. Conditions of work vary too, so check the information in the bulletins carefully. Contact Archaeology Abroad for information about subscribing to the bulletins.

HOW LONG IT WILL LAST
The minimum stay is two weeks but can be longer.

WHERE YOU CAN GO
One of about fifteen countries around the world

PAYMENT
Food and accommodation are usually provided, although you may be responsible for your own catering arrangements.

THE COST TO YOU
You will have to pay your own fares and sometimes a registration fee. Fees for field courses or training excavations can be substantial.

WHO CAN APPLY
You should normally be 18 (for insurance purposes) but occasionally digs will take you at 16. Excavation requires hard physical labour so you should be fit and healthy. Previous experience or relevant study is a bonus.

WHEN AND HOW TO APPLY
Apply to the directors of the digs as given in the bulletins.

SELECTION PROCESS
None.

PLACEMENT
You apply to the excavation you wish to attend.

TRAINING
Some excavations are especially for training and will therefore cost you fees. Others will give you training on-the-job in any case.

SUPPORT FOR PARTICIPANTS
There will be a site director and site assistants.

Austravel

Austravel specialises solely in travel to Australia and New Zealand and can give guidance and trouble-free travelling. Austravel's Great Escape is its main travel shop in London, but it has six outlets in other major UK cities. It can help you organise accommodation and arrange independent travel as well as give you information about organised trips. It can arrange flights with stopover choices, overland travel options and date-changing facilities overseas. Besides travel to Australia and New Zealand, it can arrange travel to Africa, India, South East Asia, Indonesia, the Americas, and the South Pacific.

Central Bureau for Educational Visits and Exchanges

The Central Bureau publishes a range of information guides on the theme of work, travel and exchange opportunities worldwide. It also produces a series of free information posters called the *10 Ways* series giving ideas and inspiration for seasonal work around the world, taking a gap year, going on an exchange or homestay, and ways to discover French culture and language.

Council Travel

This is the sister organisation to the Central Council on International Educational Exchanges (see chapter 10). It operates an international network of travel services for student, youth and budget travellers. On offer are discounted fares worldwide, round-the-world tickets, international rail and coach passes, low-cost accommodation, ISIC and YHA cards, travel insurance, adventure tours, and much more.

££-££££ Earthwatch

Earthwatch is an international science and education charity which recruits paying volunteers to help research scientists in fields from archaeology to zoology on short-term research projects in over fifty countries around the year. Some 3400 volunteers each year take part in the projects. Team volunteers may learn to excavate, map, photograph, observe animal behaviour, survey flora and fauna, gather ethnographical data, make collections, conduct oral history interviews, measure astronomical alignments, assist in diving operations, lend mechanical or electrical expertise, record natural sounds, and share all other field chores associated with professional expedition research.

HOW LONG IT WILL LAST
The projects last from two days to four weeks.

WHERE YOU CAN GO
Earthwatch supports projects in over fifty countries.

PAYMENT
None.

THE COST TO YOU
You pay a share of the project costs, ranging from £65 to £2495, which

includes accommodation and food costs but not travel. Education Awards: ten grants of £500 and twenty grants of £250 are being awarded annually to teachers and students to put towards the cost of joining an Earthwatch project.

WHO CAN APPLY
All English-speaking volunteers aged 17 or over are welcome. You do not usually need technical skills to take part.

WHEN AND HOW TO APPLY
Contact the Earthwatch office for an application form.

SELECTION PROCESS
There is no Selection process.

PLACEMENT
Volunteers choose their project.

TRAINING
Training is given as necessary on the project, but the work will be easy to learn and fairly straightforward.

SUPPORT FOR PARTICIPANTS
The scientist leading the project will guide and support volunteers throughout; they are well used to leading people with no previous experience.

Eurolines

Eurolines (UK) Ltd is part of the National Express group and operates scheduled coach services to continental Europe and Ireland to over 400 destinations, city centre to city centre. The coaches are modern and adhere to up-to-date safety guidelines and comforts such as on-board washroom facilities and reclining seats. Most of the services leave from London Victoria Coach Station. Eurolines offers destinations which would appeal to student travellers, for example London to Morocco via Paris. With the exception of Channel Link services or those using Stena Lynx vessels, all services to the Continent are 'through' services where the coach accompanies passengers on the ferry or Le Shuttle crossing so there is no need to disembark with luggage at the port.

There are reduced fares on most services for young people under 26. For example, a Euroline Pass offering unlimited travel across 21 countries taking in up to 48 cities in Europe costs £159 for 30 days off peak or £199 for 60 days off peak for youth travellers. Euroline tickets are valid for up to 6 months and open-dated tickets are available. All tickets, including passes, can be bought over the phone or by visiting a National Express/Eurolines agent.

North South Travel

This travel agency offers discounted air fares worldwide and full travel agency back-up. It is the only travel agency in the UK that passes on all available profits to charity. By doing so it helps to fund community projects in developing countries through the NST Development Trust (a registered charity). Projects have included development and environmental schemes in India, Sri Lanka, Israel, Uganda, Kenya, Zambia and Zimbabwe.

Although it is not geared specifically to student travel, NST believes its fares compare favourably with student travel agencies, so it is worth contacting them to find out what they can offer.

££ REMPART

REMPART aims to preserve the French cultural heritage through the restoration of threatened buildings and monuments. It consists of a grouping of more than 150 autonomous associations organising workcamps providing a wide variety of work projects involving the restoration of medieval towns, castles, churches, ancient walls, wind/watermills and industrial sites. Work includes masonry, excavations, woodwork, stone cutting, interior decorating and clearance work.

HOW LONG IT WILL LAST
Workcamps last from two to six weeks. Most of them are open during the Easter holidays and from July to September. A few camps are open throughout the year.

WHERE YOU CAN GO
France.

PAYMENT
None.

THE COST TO YOU
You will have to pay your fares to France and the site as well as FF220 for insurance and FF45–55 per day for food and accommodation. Accommodation is often in a campsite. You will also help with camp duties and should take a sleeping bag.

WHO CAN APPLY
Anyone over 14 can apply, but many sites have a minimum age of 17 or 18. Previous experience is not necessary but some knowledge of French is required.

WHEN AND HOW TO APPLY
Choose which projects to work on from three workcamp programmes published in Spring, Summer and Autumn.

SELECTION PROCESS
You apply to the project you want.

PLACEMENT
This will be at the project of your choice if there are vacancies.

TRAINING
There are many skills employed on a site. If you want to learn a particular skill, ask the site leader responsible for that particular technique. You will also have the chance during the project to specialise or follow a course to enable you to become a site leader. At a number of stages during the year, techniques and lessons are offered.

SUPPORT FOR PARTICIPANTS
There are site leaders to help you.

STA Travel

STA Travel is experienced in student and young independent travel. It has 250 offices worldwide and 20 in the UK, including branches at seventeen universities. STA specialises in round-the-world tickets, flights, accommodation, overland tours, insurance and car hire.

STA can issue you with an ISIC card or youth card which entitle you to all kinds of discounts before, during and after your trip. If you do not want to travel alone, STA arranges a variety of organised tours all over the world. If you travel alone, STA can help you arrange your trip.

Trailfinders

Trailfinders is a travel agency and information centre catering for the independent traveller who want non-'package' travel. It tailors itineraries to your specific needs and can also provide discounted flights, hotels, tours and car hire. The majority of staff are graduates and all are well-travelled and undergo intensive in-house training. Trailfinders is a highly computerised firm, which means that you can be booked and ticketed within minutes.

Trailfinders offers a complete travel service, including a one-stop travel shop at its flagship travel centre at Kensington, with its visa shop and passport service; Information Centre and travellers' library; Travel Clinic; a travel goods shop and map/book shop; and foreign exchange bureau and travellers cheques. It has offices in London, Birmingham, Bristol, Dublin, Newcastle, Glasgow and Manchester and in Australia.

Usit Campus

Usit Campus is the world's largest student travel specialists, with 51 branches across the UK. It operates in 66 countries. Usit Campus student tickets are tailor made for the needs of students and young people; they are fully flexible and refundable and are usually valid for at least a year, which is essential for longer trips. It also offers tailor-made travel insurance.

Popular options for gap year students are 'open jaw' tickets that enable you to fly into one country and out of another, often in a different country altogether – making overland travel possible between the point of arrival and the point of departure. Many long-haul airlines provide free stopovers in a country en route to your final destination, another popular option with students taking a year out. Round-the-world tickets are another way of seeing a lot in a gap year. Most are suited to travel to Australasia and not to a particular country or job.

Usit Campus staff have travelled widely and many have taken several years out. Staff are kept up to date with the options for gap year students.

SEE ALSO:

AFS, *page 86*;   WWOOF, *page 127*

EIL, *pages 49, 95*;

COURSES AND WORK EXPERIENCE IN THE UK

After completing years of study at school, the last thing on your mind will be more studying or training, especially in the UK. But there may be any number of reasons for considering it as part of a year out. One reason might be to get on-the-job training through work experience. The least attractive reason, of course, is that you need to spend part of the year retaking A-levels.

Retaking A-levels

If you do need to retake A-levels, for whatever reason, you can repeat some in November or January. But check with the board whose examinations you took in the summer about what retake subjects are available. Check with the university you want to go to see what they think about resits. Some are happy for you to try and improve your grades and will offer you the same conditional offer as before; others will only consider first-take grades.

You might be able to retake at school, otherwise your local further education college will probably offer one-year courses in the most popular A-level subjects. If you want to do a completely different subject, that should be possible too. As you will be over 18, fees will be payable but should not be more than about £100 for the year, assuming you will be living at home.

The other option for retakes is tuition at one of the private tutorial college 'crammers'. They provide one-term or one-year resits. For most people this is not really an option because the fees are so high. To retake three A-levels over one year could cost as much as £8000. You are unlikely to pay less than £3000. If you do want details about these colleges, contact the Independent Schools Information Service (see Useful Addresses).

Other options

There may be other reasons why study for at least part of your year out is an attractive choice. You may need to learn a bit more about a subject before going to college; you may want to extend your knowledge of a subject simply out of interest; your college might want you to take a course in a particular subject prior to arrival; or a new job might require knowledge that you do not have. There are many reasons why you might want to spend at least some of a year off studying.

The UK has a wide range of study opportunities. Do not overlook the obvious choice of adult education classes. They take place during the day and evening and offer a wide range of subjects with the advantage that they leave you time to earn money or pursue other interests. Alternatively your local further education (FE) college might have a part-time course that would suit you. Courses include practical, creative and traditional subjects. You can get details of evening and adult education classes from your local library or through local listings such as London's *Floodlight*. Local colleges usually produce their own adult education prospectuses. If you decide to enrol, do so early because popular courses get oversubscribed. Year-long courses usually start in September or October and continue until June or July. There are also termly courses, day schools (usually on Saturday), and weekly courses. Read *Time To Learn* for details of adult education classes throughout the UK.

There are a number of voluntary organisations that also provide adult education classes. The largest is the Workers Educational Association (WEA). Ask your library whether it runs classes in your area. The WEA organises courses in academic subjects such as English literature, local history and geology as well as general subjects such as antiques, public speaking and so on. It has a long tradition of courses in politics, economics and industrial relations for workers. The WEA will consider starting a class in your area if you can find enough people to make up a class.

Also consider specialist institutions, such as West Dean College, that offer short courses in many different activities (often creative) all the year round.

If you prefer to study at home, perhaps while working, the Open College of the Arts has distance-learning art and creative courses and the Open University has short courses as well as its degree programme.

You can study virtually anything – music, art, archaeology, horticulture – you name it, someone, somewhere will let you study it.

Private courses

You can also study many subjects such as cooking, learning a language or sports at private schools. The trouble is that with specialist and private courses you have to pay for the teaching. Some specialist courses can cost several thousand pounds. If for any reason you do want to take a particular private course, check their track record and qualifications before parting with your money. But before you turn to private tuition, consider other options such as your local further education college or adult education classes, because these are reasonably priced.

Essential skills

There are other reasons for studying a subject that might be of more immediate concern. To get work in the UK – whether during your year out, vacations, part-time while at college or after competing your education – you might well need to have skills you have not yet got. These might include keyboard skills, computer knowledge, a driving licence, secretarial skills, cooking skills, a language, or even a sports qualification. Spending at least part of your year out acquiring the necessary skills would be a worthwhile investment.

TEFL

If you intend to teach English to foreigners, a TEFL qualification is desirable. The two main standard, recognised TEFL qualifications are the Cambridge/RSA Certificate in English Language Teaching to Adults (CELTA) and the Certificate in Teaching English to Speakers of Other Languages (TESOL). Both these courses are intensive and expensive – expect to pay about £900. For most courses you must be 18, and some have higher age limits. Some TEFL colleges offer cheaper, short introductory courses or self-study options. Try International House Teacher Training, TEFL Training or the English Worldwide course at Birkbeck College. For general information about TEFL courses throughout the UK, contact The British Council.

Driving

Driving is a desirable skill wherever you work, and if you have not already passed your test you should save up enough to take lessons at your local driving school. The major driving schools such as BSM and the AA usually offer discounts for students booking a course of so many lessons, but this is still very expensive to pay in one go. The other option is to work and pay by the hour as you go. Remember that you now need to pass a theory test before you can take the practical test. There are many books to help you pass the theory test and that is something you can be revising for immediately. Local driving schools may be cheaper – ask your friends which person gave the best instruction and has the best pass rate.

Other subjects

If you are interested in doing a year's full-time course in a specialist subject such as horticulture, cooking, forestry or agriculture, check the reference section of your local library for the names and addresses of colleges that deal particularly with that subject. You will normally need to apply during your final sixth-form year. If the college cannot provide accommodation, you will have to budget for board and lodging as well as fees.

If you want to qualify in a sport, perhaps with a view to teaching it to children on holiday, contact your local sports centre or club, which will be able to tell you how to set about gaining a specific sports qualification. The official body for your sport can also tell you. If you do not know their address, ask at your local library.

Specialised courses

You can take a course for fun as well as necessity. There are many specialised courses arranged by reputable organisations for all kinds of subjects – writing, sailing or natural history, for example. The advantage is that they provide high quality well-run programmes. You might therefore want to combine a study holiday with working for part of your year out – unless you can persuade your parents that such a course is a valuable investment!

Many courses take people from 16, but most will want you to be at least 18 and a few have upper age limits. Many courses take place during school and college holidays. FE and adult education classes might take place during the day or evening. Some courses will only run in particular parts of the UK, so you may have to travel to get there. This means that unless accommodation and food costs are included in the price you will have to pay for your board.

Studying in your year out can be fun and rewarding. If you are doing it because you *have* to (perhaps it is a requirement of your university), then you may not feel so happy. But if you approach any course with an open mind and a willingness to learn, virtually anything studied can be interesting and fun. You will get out as much as you put in. And there is usually plenty of time for socialising. In fact, studying a subject together is also a good way for people of similar interests to get to know one another. It can also give you the edge when applying for work or starting a course.

The courses suggested below are residential courses of a slightly different nature which you might like to consider.

££ The Arvon Foundation

For those of you who want to improve your creative writing skills, the Arvon Foundation offers a chance to work with professional writers at one of the Foundation's three centres. The courses are residential and cover poetry, fiction, drama, writing for children, song writing, travel writing, writing for radio, screenwriting and writing for the Internet. There are also courses on starting to write. (Also see Taliesin Trust, page 145.)

141

HOW LONG IT WILL LAST
The courses last for five days.

WHERE YOU CAN GO
The Arvon Foundation has three centres – Totleigh Barton in Devon, Lumb Bank in West Yorkshire and Moniack Mhorin in Inverness-shire.

PAYMENT
None.

THE COST TO YOU
The open course fee for 2000 is £340. This covers tuition, accommodation and food. A number of grants and bursaries are available for those on low incomes, including students.

WHO CAN APPLY
Anyone over 16 is welcome.

WHEN AND HOW TO APPLY
Contact the Arvon Foundation for details of courses and dates. Apply to the appropriate centre.

SELECTION
There is no Selection process.

PLACEMENT
You can go on the course of your choice, if there is room.

TRAINING
You live and work with professional writers, who give advice and encouragement. This usually involves one-to-one tutorials, group workshops and discussions and time to write on your own.

SUPPORT FOR PARTICIPANTS
Writers and participants live and work together and share meals.

££ | BOSS (British Offshore Sailing School)

This is Britain's leading sail training school and has Royal Yachting Association (RYA) recognition. It offers a range of practical and shore-based cruising courses, from introductory level to training courses for Ocean Yachtmasters and RYA Instructors. It also has a range of one-day and weekend courses for people of all levels. While you cruise you learn about safety at sea and get a chance to master the skills of steering, changing sails, reefing, tying knots and what to do in an emergency. You live on board during the course and each night is spent in a new place. Everybody takes a turn at cooking. BOSS also specialises in women-only courses run by RYA-qualified female skippers.

HOW LONG WILL IT LAST
The length of courses varies, but as an example the RYA Competent Crew course for complete beginners lasts for three weekends or five days.

WHERE YOU CAN GO
Theory courses are based at Hamble Point Marina, Hampshire. On yacht-based courses the distances travelled depends on the course and your skills.

PAYMENT
None.

THE COST TO YOU
The costs vary according to the type of course. As an example, a five-day RYA Competent Crew course costs about £390 in the main season. You sleep on board and food is provided. Sleeping bags and waterproof 'oilskins' are available for hire.

WHO CAN APPLY
There are women-only courses. No skills are necessary for the introductory courses. For more advanced courses you will need to have specified experience or qualifications.

WHEN AND HOW TO APPLY
Contact BOSS for a brochure.

SELECTION
There is no Selection process.

PLACEMENT
You will be placed on the course you book for, subject to the maximum number of places available.

TRAINING
BOSS is run by a team of highly qualified instructors.

SUPPORT FOR PARTICIPANTS
BOSS aims to make sailing exciting, enjoyable, fun and above all safe.

The Duke of Edinburgh's Award

This does not offer gap year opportunities as such, but is included here because many opportunities in this book can be used to complete part of an Award. This particularly applies to some of the expeditions and challenges (see chapter 11). If you particularly want to take an Award, ask the organisation you are interested in if it is licensed to operate the Award.

The Award scheme consists of a voluntary, non-competitive programme of leisure activities for those aged 14–25 designed to offer a personal and individual challenge. The programme has four sections: service, skills, expeditions and physical recreation, all at three levels: Bronze, Silver and Gold.

For the Gold level only, there is also a residential project. You must have completed your awards by your 25th birthday. About 400 organisations are licensed to operate the Award. Your entrance pack will cost less than a CD, and Award costs after that will depend on what you choose to do and what is available locally.

£-££

The Field Studies Council (FSC)

The FSC is an independent educational charity that aims to increase environmental awareness and understanding. There are eleven well-equipped centres where you can learn about every aspect of the country-side and wildlife, and there are hundreds of courses available. The FSC also arranges overseas tours.

HOW LONG IT WILL LAST
Courses usually last for a weekend or a week. Overseas tours are typically longer.

WHERE YOU CAN GO.
The centres are in England and Wales.

PAYMENT
None.

THE COST TO YOU
Request a free copy of the *FSC Courses* brochure for details of prices. For overseas tours, ask for the *FSC Overseas Experiences* brochure. Prices start at around £106 for a weekend and £257 for a week.

WHO CAN APPLY
The FSC provides opportunities for everyone – whether under 8 or over 80.

SELECTION
There is no Selection process.

PLACEMENT
Apply for the course you want to do.

TRAINING
Teaching is done by permanent staff and visiting experts.

SUPPORT FOR PARTICIPANTS
The FSC employs experienced staff.

££

Outward Bound

Outward Bound provides challenging outdoor experiences which promote personal development. Outward Bound provide the environment, equipment, instruction and support. There is also a women-only course. Some of the courses are designated for the Duke of Edinburgh's Award.

Activities depend on the age group and length and type of course, but a centre-based course may include activities such as rock climbing, canoeing, abseilling, hill walking, camping, orienteering, high-challenge activities and team dynamics. Accommodation is in shared, single-sex bedrooms with at least one night away from the centre.

HOW LONG IT WILL LAST
The courses can last from a weekend to 19 days.

WHERE YOU CAN GO
England, Scotland, Wales.

PAYMENT
None.

THE COST TO YOU
This varies according to the type and length of course but a typical price is around £500 for a twelve-day course. This includes all tuition, meals, basic accident insurance, transport during the programme, accommodation and all specialist equipment and clothing. If you are aged between 11 and 24 and could not otherwise afford to attend, you might be eligible for an Outward Bound scholarship or bursary. Alternatively, support might be available from a local Outward Bound Association.

WHO CAN APPLY
There are courses for people from age 16 upwards and courses particularly aimed at people aged 19–24.

WHEN AND HOW TO APPLY
Ask for a brochure from Outward Bound.

SELECTION PROCESS
None.

TRAINING
Instruction is given by qualified staff.

SUPPORT FOR PARTICIPANTS
Each instructor holds a first-aid certificate together with an appropriate National Governing Body qualification and will have taken the Outward Bound's rigorous passing-out procedure before being allowed to lead any activity. Participants aged 11–24 get a one-to-one discussion with the course tutor and then together you write a report summarising your experience.

££ Taliesin Trust

This is a residential writer's centre which operates in a similar way to the Arvon Foundation (see above). It was created by the Taliesin Trust with the support of the Arts Council of Wales. The wide range of courses aim to encourage writing in both English and Welsh.

HOW LONG IT WILL LAST
Most courses run from Monday evening to Saturday morning.

WHERE YOU CAN GO
The centre is at Tŷ Newydd in Wales.

PAYMENT
None.

THE COST TO YOU
A Monday to Saturday course costs £330 inclusive for a single room; a weekend course costs £135. Shared rooms are cheaper. People on low incomes may be eligible for a bursary.

WHO CAN APPLY
Everyone over the age of 16 is welcome.

WHEN AND HOW TO APPLY
You need to book for a course as early as possible, so contact Taliesin Trust well in advance for details of courses and dates.

SELECTION
There is no Selection process.

PLACEMENT
You can attend the course you apply for, subject to the maximum number of places – 16 per course.

TRAINING
Each course has two tutors who are working writers.

SUPPORT FOR PARTICIPANTS
Tutors and participants live and work together.

Work experience

An alternative to study or casual employment is specific work experience. This combines training and experience of a particular job with financial remuneration. You do a real job under the guidance of more experienced workers and gain a real insight into aspects of a specific career. Although much of the training is on the job, you are usually given time for structured study or instruction. Three examples of established work experience schemes are given below.

Army – Gap Year Commission (GYC)

The army can offer from four to eighteen months' employment especially for gap students in the form of a Gap Year Commission. After three weeks' training, you are placed in a regiment and given responsibility as an officer. The experience is designed to broaden your horizons and prepare you for the challenges of university and whatever career you choose. It also gives you the chance to gain an impression of the army, either with view to joining or simply as a gap year experience. Regiments and Corps accepting GYC officers include the Household Cavalry (not women), Royal Artillery, Royal Signals, Royal Logistic Corps, Adjutant general's Corps, Royal Armoured Corps (not women), Royal Engineers, Infantry (not women), Royal Electrical and Mechanical Engineers.

HOW LONG IT WILL LAST
From four to eighteen months.

WHERE YOU WILL GO
Wherever your participating Regiment or Corps is based.

PAYMENT
Your salary will start at £11,793, rising to £12,609 after nine months.

THE COST TO YOU
None.

WHO CAN APPLY
You must have a confirmed place on a degree course at a UK university or college, with all exams completed before entry to Sandhurst. You must also be aged 18 but under 20 on the day of commissioning, be recommended by your headteacher, unmarried, accepted by the Corps or Regiment of your choice, passed by the Army Medical Board, and have passed the regular Commissions Board with a specific recommendation for GYC.

WHEN AND HOW TO APPLY
Apply well before the start of the Sandhurst courses in October and March annually. Contact your Army Careers Adviser (Officer) through your school's career staff or phone for information (see Useful Addresses).

SELECTION PROCESS
This takes place at the Regular Commissions Board (RCB) at Westbury in Wiltshire and a very high standard is expected. It lasts three and a half days and you will receive a full briefing before attending the board. For most activities you will be part of a group of eight. You will take intelligence tests and a written test on your knowledge of world affairs and write an essay. Your communication skills are assessed through group discussions, by giving a short lecture and taking part in a 'planning project' to assess your

ability to devise and present logical solutions. Leadership skills are assessed through outdoor tasks and you will be given a command task to carry out with your group. You need to be fit, although physical fitness is not specifically tested. You will also be given a series of interviews.

PLACEMENT
Your placement will be with the Corps or Regiment of your choice, if they accept you.

TRAINING
This takes place at Sandhurst and lasts three weeks. It covers such things as map reading, skill at arms, signals and drill, as well as battlecraft exercises. There will also be room and kit inspections, assault courses, initiative tests, weapon training and sessions on various relevant topics.

SUPPORT FOR PARTICIPANTS
You will receive the support that the army provides for all its personnel.

The Year in Industry

The Year in Industry gives high-calibre students a pre-degree taste of industry in their gap year. It places students in companies where they do challenging paid work and also provides comprehensive 'off the job' training. The scheme benefits both employers and students, and over 250 companies take part. Although students from all disciplines are welcome, most places are science- or technology-based.

HOW LONG IT WILL LAST
The scheme runs annually from mid-August to mid-July, but the exact dates vary between regions and companies.

WHERE YOU WILL GO
The Year in Industry scheme involves British companies.

PAYMENT
Salary rates vary from company to company, but you will normally be paid the typical rate for 18 year old employees, subject to The Year in Industry recommendation of £140 per week. Typically you will work 35–37 hours per week.

THE COST TO YOU
There is no cost to you, but you are responsible for finding your own accommodation. Some companies arrange to sponsor their students for their degree course.

WHO CAN APPLY
The scheme is specifically for gap year students who want to find out more about industry and what a career in industry entails. You must be 18 or 19 and have just taken your A-levels, BTEC or equivalent, and must have a confirmed offer of a degree course.

WHEN AND HOW TO APPLY

Complete a registration form obtained from The Year in Industry address and send it to your first choice region as listed on the form. The form will be copied to employers. You must ask your school or college to send a copy of your UCAS Reference under a separate cover. Your profile will be passed to interested companies.

SELECTION PROCESS

Companies look for good exam grades but also take non-academic achievements into consideration. After reading the profiles and application forms, companies select candidates for interview and you may be asked to attend several. Some companies decide at the beginning of the year, but interviews continue throughout the spring and summer. If you have not been placed by the end of May, your application will go into the national clearing system to give you a chance of an interview in another region. Once you have accepted a place, you must give a firm commitment in writing to the company and withdraw from other interviews.

PLACEMENT

You will usually be placed with a local company unless you prefer to work away from home. The Year in Industry will try to place you. If that is not possible, you will be considered for other regions through the national clearing system if you indicate your consent on the registration form. The Year in Industry will try to match you with a company which will give you relevant experience, but cannot guarantee a place with a specific company. It will follow up any contacts you may already have in a company of your choice. You can choose whether or not to accept a particular interview or job offer.

TRAINING

You will receive up to 20–25 days' formal 'off the job' training in the form of short courses at residential college in three periods of one week, one of which is a compulsory pre-placement induction course. You will be asked to complete training assignments and be subject to continuous assessment and performance appraisals. Students are asked to complete a special project to be presented at the end of the year.

SUPPORT FOR PARTICIPANTS

During your placement you will have access to scheme tutors who will help you with your training assignments, appraisals and keeping a record of your work and training as evidence for professional and vocational qualifications. Your Year in Industry Regional Director or Industrial Tutor will also give information and guidance.

Courses abroad

COURSES ABROAD

Going to another country has its advantages when it comes to learning. Studying abroad can give you a different perspective on your studies, and at the same time you can discover a different culture at first hand as well as developing essential language skills. Language students, in particular, benefit from language courses abroad. The chance to learn a language with native speakers and to practise by living with and talking to people in the country of the language you are learning is invaluable. People who do study languages abroad testify to the improvement it gives to their language skills.

There are other courses which benefit from study in another country – art, architecture, history and archaeology are just some of them. These have a direct input from the country concerned. For example, where better to study the art and architecture of Italy than in Italy itself?

But other courses are studied abroad. For some university students, several months or a year abroad, perhaps with the ERASMUS scheme, is an integral part of their course. Not only do they learn their subject, but it is conducted in the language of the country. So they learn not only their subject but the language as well. Gap year students who want to brush up their language skills or improve their knowledge in a subject which lends itself to foreign teaching will benefit too. The advantages of studying abroad are a better understanding of a country, its people and its language, and a sense of independence as well as the practical skills learnt.

One problem with studying abroad is the cost. Language tuition while staying with a family as a paying guest for a few weeks may be reasonable, but some of the extended institutional art or language courses can be very expensive, as can spending a year at an overseas university. If it is too expensive but you nevertheless think it is important to you, you may have to work first to get the money or settle for a shorter course. Another disadvantage with some courses is that if you stay with a family rather than attending a central course with other students, you may feel rather isolated.

Some families accept young people as young as fourteen as paying guests and give language tuition, but for most the lower age limit is sixteen or eighteen. Before you choose a course, check what the age group of the majority of students is likely to be. Although most cater for a particular range, some accept people of all ages and you may prefer to be with people of more or less your own age.

To apply for a study course, contact the institution named and check that you satisfy the criteria laid down. For study at American universities, for example, you may need references from your teachers or other responsible people, so make sure that they are willing to provide these. Apply in good time, and on school exchanges be prepared to accept the placing you are offered.

You do not need to have any particular skills if you are taking a beginner's course in a language, say, but other courses may require a grounding, perhaps at A-level standard, in a language. For academic exchanges you should be able to offer a good academic record and show that you are willing and adaptable and preferably have some outside interests.

Study in the EU

As a national of a member state, you may study and undergo training anywhere in the European Union. This has been made much easier in the last few years by the introduction of the right of residence for students and programmes such as ERASMUS (see below). You may apply to study anywhere in the Union. If you want to be accepted by a European educational establishment, though, you might need to have some knowledge of the language as a . 'ition of acceptance.

If you want to study in a member state for *less* than three months, for example on a language course, then all you need is a valid passport. In some member states you might be required to register with the local authorities. If you want to study in a member state other than your own for *more* than three months, you must be enrolled at an approved educational establishment, be covered by adequate health insurance, and have sufficient means to prevent you becoming a burden on the social security system of that state. If you satisfy these conditions, the host state will issue you with an EU residence permit. If the course lasts less than a year, the permit will be valid for the duration of your course. If it lasts over a year, the permit will be valid for a year but renewable annually. In your case, as a gap year student, you will be unlikely to be studying abroad for more than a year.

The European Commission has a number of programmes which enable young people to study abroad. But you cannot apply to them directly. If you are interested, ask your teacher, lecturer or youth worker to contact the schemes on your behalf. They can get more information from The

British Council (see Useful Addresses). The schemes are Leonardo Da Vinci, LINGUA, SOCRATES-ERASMUS, and Youth For Europe.

Leonardo Da Vinci Programme

This is another programme that might interest older students who want to spend time abroad either during or after higher education. The Leonardo Da Vinci Programme implements vocational training policies in EU member states. It can provide opportunities for industrial training for undergraduates and recent graduates with companies in Europe for between three and twelve months. Apply via your college or university.

LINGUA

The LINGUA programme enables young people aged 14–25 in general, vocational or technical training to work with a group of students in another European country in a joint project which involves learning another language. It promotes less widely used and taught languages such as Danish, Finnish, Portuguese, Greek, etc.

SOCRATES-ERASMUS

Many universities now take part in the SOCRATES-ERASMUS Programme, which arranges exchanges to enable students to study part of their degree abroad for between three and twelve months. You could, therefore, depending on your university and course, spend up to a year of your course abroad. SOCRATES-ERASMUS may supply financial support for travel costs, language courses and differences in the cost of living. You would continue to receive any student loan to which you are entitled and will be exempt from tuition fees at the *host* institution. So if you would like to study abroad but cannot afford to spend the gap year doing so, the SOCRATES-ERASMUS Programme is something you might be able to pursue once you are in higher education.

Your university must recognise that your period of study abroad is an integral part of its study programme, and that it replaces a comparable period in the home university even if the content of the programme differs. This includes exams and other forms of assessment. For further information, look at the UK SOCRATES-ERASMUS website.

Youth for Europe (Youth Exchange Centre)

The Youth Exchange Centre (YEC) promotes exchanges in the UK and overseas. The YEC is a department of the British Council and is also the UK national agency for the European Union's Youth for Europe programme. Youth exchanges in general are open to people aged 15–25 who are members of an organisation. However, within the Youth for Europe programme, the YEC can give support to young people who themselves create a local project (Youth Initiatives) or who take part in voluntary service for three months to a year. It is aimed at people who would not otherwise have had a chance to travel.

£££££

American Scandinavian Student Exchange (ASSE) – International Student Exchange Programmes

ASSE arranges an exchange programme for students wishing to spend a school year abroad. You live as a member of the community and attend a local school. For extra payments, trips around the host country can be arranged.

HOW LONG IT WILL LAST
A school year. Students going to North America and Europe leave in August and return the following June. For Australia and New Zealand the dates are from January to the following August or December.

WHERE YOU CAN GO
You can spend your school year in the USA, Canada (French- and English-speaking), France, Germany, Australia, Japan, Scandinavia, Spain, Italy, Switzerland, Slovakia, South Africa, Poland, Thailand, Taiwan and China.

THE COST TO YOU
The cost of the return air fares is included in the costs to North America (including internal flights). In French-speaking Canada, the cost includes an intensive language course at the beginning of the year. Travel to European destinations is not included. You will need pocket money and personal expenses.

WHO CAN APPLY
You must be having your sixteenth, seventeenth or eighteenth birthday during your year abroad for the USA and English-speaking Canada, or your sixteenth or seventeenth birthday for French-speaking Canada. For New

Zealand or Australia you must be 16 or 17 or, if you are 18, must not turn 19 before 1 July during your year abroad.

WHEN AND HOW TO APPLY
Complete the application form and questionnaire in the ASSE brochure and send them together with a registration fee (included in the total cost) and a copy of your latest school report. Your form tutor or another teacher who knows you must complete the school reference form and return it completed in the addressed envelope.

SELECTION PROCESS
When ASSE has received the above documents, you will be called to an interview. Your suitability will be decided on the basis of all the above.

SUPPORT FOR PARTICIPANTS
You will get support from your host family. ASSE also has area representatives who keep in close contact with students by means of meetings throughout the year.

££-£££££ | Art History Abroad

AHA organises a variety of carefully structured courses for people who want to study the artistic heritage of Italy. As well as specialist courses for students taking the History of Art A-level, it arranges longer trips, which travel between major cultural centres, for gap year students. The course for gap students is the Spring course which runs each year for six weeks from the last week in January and aims to give a comprehensive overview of Italian art and culture. It includes a preparatory course in London and takes 24 students. The A-level revision course lasts one week during the Easter holiday. The Summer course in the first two weeks of August is open to sixth formers and school-leavers.

HOW LONG IT WILL LAST
The course aimed specifically at gap students lasts six weeks, but there are also two-week summer courses.

WHERE YOU CAN GO
Italy: the Spring 'gap' course takes in Venice, Bologna, Florence, Siena and Rome.

THE COST TO YOU
At the time of writing prices were: Spring 'gap' course: £3800 for six weeks; and the Summer course: £1600 for two weeks. The prices include everything except food. You are advised to take enough money for daily food and occasional spending.

WHO CAN APPLY
The Spring course is aimed at gap students, the Easter course at A-level students and the Summer courses at upper sixth, school-leavers or gap students. The age range is 17–21.

WHEN AND HOW TO APPLY

Apply on the registration form accompanying the AHA brochure with a passport size photo and the specified deposit. The balance must be paid eight weeks before the course starts.

SUPPORT FOR PARTICIPANTS

Tutors stay in the same hotels to be on call 24 hours a day on all student courses. There is one experienced tutor per eight students.

£££

The British Institute of Florence

The British Institute of Florence has been the city's focal point for Anglo-Italian cultural cooperation since 1917. Its main functions today are the teaching of general and business English to Italians and of the Italian language and culture to students from abroad. A typical programme consists of Italian language lessons, including alternating lecture courses on Italian art history, cookery or drawing. There are also shorter courses and another centre at Massa Marittima.

HOW LONG IT WILL LAST

Most of the Institute's courses run for two or four weeks, but gap students typically take courses lasting two successive months starting in September or January. Shorter courses are also available.

WHERE YOU CAN GO

The main centre is at Florence, Italy, with another at Massa Marittima.

THE COST TO YOU

Language lesson prices are about £255 for a standard beginner's four-week course or £370 for higher-level courses. Four weeks of art history lessons would cost an extra £220. Accommodation and food are extra and the Institute can advise and make bookings for you in Italian homes, pensioni and hotels. Don't forget to allow for fares to Italy.

WHO CAN APPLY

The Institute generally takes students from 16+, but can take younger students by arrangement with parents.

WHEN AND HOW TO APPLY

Contact the Institute for up-to-date details of courses, dates and costs. To book your place on a course, send your deposit with your application.

SELECTION

Except for A-level courses and 'fast track' courses for professional people, there are no formal entry requirements.

PLACEMENT

If you already have some knowledge of Italian, you will be placed at the appropriate level on the basis on an initial interview and test.

TRAINING

Italian is taught by well qualified and experienced Italian staff who also speak English. The Institute can also call on distinguished visiting university lecturers.

SUPPORT FOR PARTICIPANTS

Regular receptions are held so that English and Italian students studying at the Institute can meet. The Institute has a library at the Palazzo Landfredini in Florence which students can use. This is also the base for the Institute's emerging Centre of Art History, which aims to serve the needs of student visitors, including gap year students, who need a study base in the city.

££-£££££ | Council on International Educational Exchange (CIEE)

The Council is a non-profit, non-governmental organisation that aims to develop international activities and programmes that will help people gain understanding, acquire knowledge, and develop skills for living in a globally interdependent and culturally diverse world.

The opportunities available include international study opportunities and work programmes, many of which are open to gap year students. Study courses include languages, area studies, semester and year study opportunities and arts, business and environmental studies. It also offers work placements (see chapter 10).

Courses can last up to a year, depending on where you go. The cost of study programmes varies according to where you go and the length of stay. Many of the study courses include all tuition, meals, accommodation, insurance, emergency support, academic counselling and ISIC. Travel costs for work and study placements are extra.

A few of the language courses take people from 16+ and A-level students, but most are for gap students or undergraduates and above. Some of the courses require an appropriate A-level.

Contact CIEE for application forms and details of specific courses. For international study programmes, the deadline is two to four weeks before departure. For specialised study courses, the deadline is 1 April or 1 November, depending on whether you are going for the Spring semester or the Fall semester/academic year.

£ | En Famille Overseas

En Famille arranges visits to host families for people of all ages who want to improve their knowledge of a foreign language. There are two types of visit: a study holiday with language lessons or an individual stay. En Famille often arrange stays for language students in their year out. The stays can be for any length of time, from one week or up to a year with a family.

WHERE YOU CAN GO
France, Germany, Spain or Italy.

THE COST TO YOU
Study holidays cost £288 for a week for full board in Paris or £319 for a week in the Provinces. These are for intensive private tuition with the host or hostess. If you choose to study at a Tours language school and stay with a family nearby, the cost is about £496 for two weeks for teenagers. Travel costs are extra. The Loire coaching centre takes four girls at A-level for two weeks for £642. A language tuition week in Germany costs £529.

WHO CAN APPLY
For the study holidays you must be 14 or over for individual tuition, or 16 or over for a language school course.

WHEN AND HOW TO APPLY
En Famille can arrange visits at any time of the year. Apply as early as possible on the application form from En Famille and enclose two small photographs of yourself plus an enrolment fee of £30 (non-refundable but valid for three seasons). There is also a selection and booking fee of £29.

SELECTION PROCESS
There are no selection criteria but En Famille recommends that students should have studied the language, preferably for a minimum of two years.

PLACEMENT
En Famille carefully matches applicants and host families.

SUPPORT FOR PARTICIPANTS
You will have support from the host family and, at Tours, a local organiser.

£££££ The English Speaking Union (ESU)

The ESU promotes international understanding and human achievement through widening the use of the English language throughout the world. It offers forty young people the Secondary School Exchange Scholarship, which involves two or three academic terms at a North American private boarding school. There are two types of scholarship: one for the full academic year of three terms September to June, the other for two terms January to June. Applicants are welcome from state and independent schools.

HOW LONG IT WILL LAST
Two or three academic terms.

WHERE YOU CAN GO
North America.

THE COST TO YOU
The ESU scholarship provides free tuition and board; all other costs must be met by you – about £2000.

WHO CAN APPLY
You must be British and have taken your A-levels or the equivalent and be under 19 years 6 months when you take up the scholarship.

WHEN AND HOW TO APPLY
Write for an application form from the Awards Manager enclosing a large stamped, addressed envelope. Applications should be returned by the end of January for the three-term scholarship (interviews in February) and by mid-September for the two-term scholarship (interviews in October). Shortlisting takes place immediately after the closing date and you will be advised in writing.

SELECTION PROCESS
The selection panel is composed of headteachers. It looks for academic strength (but not necessarily brilliance) and, just as importantly, extracurricular achievement and ambassadorial qualities.

PLACEMENT
Your preferences with regard to area, subjects taught, etc, will be passed on to the programme organisers in the host countries, but there are no guarantees of allocation to a particular school. Scholars are expected to accept the school to which they have been allocated.

SUPPORT FOR PARTICIPANTS
Students are met at their destinations by a representative from their school or the ESU.

££–£££££ | Euro-Academy Ltd

Euro-Academy arranges language courses and home stays abroad. Home stays allow you to take a full part in the life of the country visited. The courses include vacation courses, long-term courses and individual tuition. Diploma courses provide students with a language qualification. In Italy there are academic semesters and courses in painting or photography.

HOW LONG IT WILL LAST
The long-term courses from eight or twelve weeks in France, Germany and Spain are specifically aimed at gap year students. Other courses last for a vacation, an academic semester or a year. Intensive courses last two or three weeks.

WHERE YOU CAN GO
Courses are available in France, Germany, Italy, Spain, Ecuador, Portugal and Russia.

THE COST TO YOU
Prices vary from, for example, about £310 for seven days' home stay in Nice, exclusive of travel, to £1440 for Spanish tuition for 12 weeks with half-board accommodation, exclusive of travel. The costs vary depending on the place, length and type of course. Travel, and sometimes accommodation, is extra. You must also have travel insurance.

WHO CAN APPLY
The age of participants varies depending on the place and nature of stay. Ages for home stays can be from as young as 12 up to 25 years. The age for courses varies; some take 16 year olds, but the university and senior courses usually have a minimum age of 18.

WHEN AND HOW TO APPLY
There are courses throughout the year. Apply with the form in the Euro-Academy brochure. The insurance premium, a photo and £100 deposit must accompany the form.

SUPPORT FOR PARTICIPANTS
A local coordinator ensures regular monitoring of host families and super-vises the programme at the centre. There is no permanent resident repre-sentative for university centres, but assistance can be provided by University Course Organisers.

££-£££££ | European Educational Opportunities Programme

This organisation arranges home-stay and study courses in the USA and Europe. Gap year students will be particularly interested in the College Campus and College Host Family programmes in the USA. For College Campus you stay in a college dormitory. On the College Host Family pro-gramme you stay with a family close to your college.

HOW LONG IT WILL LAST
You stay a semester or a year.

WHERE YOU CAN GO
USA.

THE COST TO YOU
The College Host Family programme costs about £3487 for a semester and £4692 for an academic year. College programme fees include college fees, food and accommodation. Flights cost extra.

WHO CAN APPLY
You must be 18+ for the College Campus programme and 18–21 for the College Host Family programme.

WHEN AND HOW TO APPLY
Apply to EEOP for the application and registration forms and send them

with the registration fee by 15 April for an August/September start or by 30 September to start in January.

PLACEMENT
When your application has been received, EEOP will invite you to an interview.

SUPPORT FOR PARTICIPANTS
You receive personal help, support and advice from your programme co-ordinators during the year.

£

The European Union Youth Orchestra

If you have a talent for music the European Youth Orchestra could offer you the chance to work with expert instrumental professors and to perform in the great concert halls of the world. The orchestra fills 140 places annually and auditions take place in each of the EU counties. If successful, you would take part in a rehearsal period followed by a tour of up to ten concerts. As well as preparing the repertoire for the forthcoming tour, the rehearsal period offers opportunities for chamber music, sport and other recreational and social activities.

HOW LONG IT WILL LAST
The rehearsal period lasts two weeks, followed by the tour.

WHERE YOU CAN GO
Rehearsal periods and tour venues vary each year but take place in Europe.

PAYMENT
You will not receive a fee, but tuition, travel and full-board accommodation are provided free of charge.

THE COST TO YOU
You have to pay our own travel expenses to auditions.

WHO CAN APPLY
You must have a passport from one of the EU countries, be aged 14–23 and be at least grade 8 in your chosen orchestral instrument. Even current members have to audition every year, so competition is high.

WHEN AND HOW TO APPLY
Contact the EUYO for an application form and details of auditions. If you are not a current member of the EUYO, you will need to supply two written references of musical ability.

SELECTION
Selection is by audition and there are two stages – preliminaries and finals.

PLACEMENT
Successful candidates become members of the EUYO and will be invited to take part in the forthcoming tours.

TRAINING
During the rehearsal period you will work in tutti rehearsals and in sectionals with tutors from leading orchestras in Europe.

SUPPORT FOR PARTICIPANTS
The EUYO is organised by the International Youth Foundation of Great Britain.

££££

Goethe Institut

The Goethe Institut offers German language courses. You can take German courses at any level, from complete beginners onwards. Most teaching is done in classes but tutoring for small groups can be arranged. You can, if you wish, study for and take any of the exams offered by the Institut.

HOW LONG IT WILL LAST
Courses last two, four or eight weeks.

WHERE YOU CAN GO
Fifteen towns throughout Germany.

THE COST TO YOU
Typical prices are about DM3170 for an eight-week course of 24 lessons a week or DM1690 for a four-week course. Accommodation is extra and brings the cost of an eight-week course to about DM4750 in a single room or DM4570 sharing. Single-room accommodation is limited. Accommodation is in student dormitories or in private homes. There is an additional fee for examinations.

WHO CAN APPLY
You must be at least 18, unless attending a youth course.

WHEN AND HOW TO APPLY
There are courses throughout the year. Contact the Institut for an application form and details of courses and dates. Apply preferably at least four weeks before the starting date of your chosen course. Upon confirmation, an initial payment is due.

SELECTION
Preliminary placement in a particular course level is based on a test in the application form. A test on the day of arrival determines your final course level.

SUPPORT FOR PARTICIPANTS
The eight-week intensive course includes social and cultural programmes and activities. There are excellent cultural programmes and recreational activities throughout the year.

£££££

Youth for Understanding UK

YFU is an international educational exchange organisation that provides the opportunity of a structured academic programme abroad. You will stay with a Youth for Understanding host family and attend high school for an academic year or a semester (six months) near to where your host family stays. It is just the country, culture and language that varies. To make the experience a 'family' one and to help everyone become international and culturally aware, YFU asks that your family accepts a student to stay – not a direct exchange.

HOW LONG IT WILL LAST
You will usually stay for an academic year. For most students the exchange year lasts from August to July. In Japan the school year runs from March to January. For some countries shorter programmes are available.

WHERE YOU CAN GO
The countries included in the exchange programme are Argentina, Australia, Belarus, Benelux (Belgium, Netherlands, Luxembourg), Brazil, Canada, Chile, Colombia, the Czech and Slovak Republics, Denmark, Ecuador, Estonia, Finland, France, Germany, Greece, Hungary, Italy, Japan, Kazakhstan, Korea, Latvia, Lithuania, Mexico, New Zealand, Norway, Paraguay, Philippines, Poland, Romania, Russia, South Africa, Spain, Sweden, Switzerland, Ukraine, Uruguay, Venezuela and USA.

THE COST TO YOU
Programmes cost between £3000 and £4000 for the year stay. Ask the YFU office for details of costs for the programme in which you are interested. Scholarships are available for the YFU's 'Encounter Japan' programme and these are competed for each year on submission of an essay and interviews. The scholarships are also available to the grandchildren of Japanese POWs.

WHO CAN APPLY
The programme is for 16–18 year old students with an upper limit of turning 19 when on the programme.

WHEN AND HOW TO APPLY
Application details vary according to the programme you choose. Contact the YFU office for details. If you are applying for an 'Encounter Japan' scholarship, the closing date for essays is September for going to Japan the following March.

SELECTION PROCESS
Places are awarded to applicants who show maturity, open-mindedness and the desire to live and learn in a new culture.

TRAINING

You will receive full training to help you fit into your new life. There is ongoing training while on a programme and on return.

SUPPORT FOR PARTICIPANTS

You will be fully supported by the YFU office in the country you are visiting, with assistance from your host family and school.

SEE ALSO:

EIL, *pages 49, 95*

Challenges and expeditions

If you want adventure and to test yourself to the limit, then consider going on an expedition or taking part in a challenge-type activity. These come in many forms – they could be courses, adventure holidays or research expeditions. Holidays overseas have been covered in chapter 8, so this chapter concentrates on challenges and expeditions, many of which take place in remote parts of the world.

Many of these type of activities are organised by reputable scientific associations which want to encourage people to take an interest in the world about them, as well as get some help for their projects. Participants are expected to be physically fit in often demanding conditions and to be open to the challenges of living rough and working in out-of-the-way places. You might be recording lion spoors or counting flowers – whatever it is, it is part of a rigorous scientific project and needs to be treated seriously. Many people like the idea of contributing to human knowledge while taking part in a challenging lifestyle.

Some activities are purely designed to test you physically and to give you experience of far flung places. Challenges often fall into this category – whether you crew a tall ship or take part in an overland trek.

You are expected to be responsible, reliable, hard working and ready to contribute to the team as a whole. You quickly learn to stretch yourself to your limits and become more mature. It is also a wonderful way to see a part of the world which you never have had a chance to visit otherwise.

These kinds of activities give you the chance to live in unusual conditions with a group of people with whom you must get on well. However, you cannot give up in the middle if you find it tough going, unless it is a matter of life or death, because you are an integral part of a team. If you are not the kind of person who gets on with other people and can rough it, then these activities are not for you.

The minimum age is usually 18, and usually no special skills are required. Only occasionally are particular skills needed, so read the application forms carefully. The one big disadvantage is the cost, which can run into thousands of pounds for an expedition in a far-off part of the world. You normally finance your own place, so you might need to spend one or two years raising the money in your spare time.

££–£££££ | Brathay Exploration Group

Brathay Exploration Group has been running expeditions and courses for over fifty years, both abroad and in the UK. It offers you the chance to increase your environmental and cultural understanding through adventure, exploration and personal development projects.

HOW LONG IT WILL LAST
Expeditions typically run from one to six weeks, and training courses in such things as mountain skills, mountain first aid and Nordic skiing last about one week.

WHERE YOU CAN GO
Recent destinations include Northern India, Belize, Svalbard, Alaska, Mongolia, Morocco, Norway, the French Alps and Scotland.

PAYMENT
None.

THE COST TO YOU
The cost ranges from £295 to £2350, depending on the destination and length of the expedition. A typical training course costs about £200. Expedition fees include all travel costs from the meeting point, all food and accommodation during the expedition period, comprehensive insurance and all safety, and scientific and group camping equipment. Included in the overall cost is a deposit of £60 to £350, depending on the expedition. If you cannot afford the full cost Brathay have some grants available and can give advice about fundraising.

WHO CAN APPLY
The age range is from 16 to 25 years. Wherever possible, no medical condition or handicap is a bar to taking part.

WHEN AND HOW TO APPLY
Apply as early as possible. Complete the application form in the Brathay brochure and return it with the relevant deposit. This will be returned if you cannot join the expedition of your choice.

SELECTION PROCESS
Selection is made on the basis of information given on the application form. This is forwarded to the team leader who is responsible for allocating places.

PLACEMENT
If possible, you will be given a place on the expedition of your choice.

TRAINING
You will learn on the expedition and can undertake specific training on Brathay courses designed to assist the development of the group's own leaders.

SUPPORT FOR PARTICIPANTS
The expeditions are run by volunteer leaders with proven ability and enthusiasm, who also contribute to the cost of their venture.

£££££–£££££ | British Schools Exploring Society

This UK-based charity provides opportunities for young people to take part in exploratory projects in remote regions, led by experts from universities, schools, the medical professions, the Services and industry. The expeditions give you the chance to combine the excitement of living under testing conditions with the research and production of valuable scientific work.

HOW LONG IT WILL LAST
Expeditions last about six weeks, mid-July to August, or three to four months, usually beginning in the Spring. There is a special 'gap year' expedition.

WHERE YOU CAN GO
Recent expeditions have been planned to Iceland, Malawi and North India.

PAYMENT
None.

THE COST TO YOU
From £1500 to £3000.

WHO CAN APPLY
You must be between 16 and 20 at the time of application, and in or between full-time education. BSES looks for enthusiasm, determination, common sense, the ability to work in a team, physical fitness and a sense of humour. It is important that you have a basic knowledge of camping, hill walking and outdoor activities in general, but there are opportunities whatever your abilities. People with physical disabilities are welcome, but due to the nature of the expeditions must have full walking mobility.

WHEN AND HOW TO APPLY
Send an A4 stamped, addressed envelope to BSES for an application form. Selection weekends for the three- to four-month expeditions are held in late Autumn, so apply well before that. Apply by the end of October for the summer expeditions.

SELECTION PROCESS

The aim is not to select an elite group, but people who will benefit from and contribute to the experience. After initial screening of the application forms, everyone who is short-listed will be called for interview at the Society's London office or a regional centre. Final selection will be completed as soon as possible, to give you the maximum time to raise the cost. Selection for the gap year expedition involves a weekend when applicants will be chosen for their suitability for that particular expedition.

PLACEMENT

Placement on the expedition of your choice will depend on the Selection process.

TRAINING

You attend a briefing, usually during the Easter break – either two or three days at a camp site in the Peak District or a day at the Royal Geographical Society, depending on the needs of the expedition. People attending the Hathersage camp site will learn new outdoor skills. Expedition members also receive regular mailings between January and the departure date.

SUPPORT FOR PARTICIPANTS

BSES can deal with individual queries and problems.

£££-£££££ | Coral Cay Conservation

Volunteers with Coral Cay come from all over the world and help provide countries with the information they need to properly manage and protect their coastal environment. It organises many expeditions to Honduras and the Philippines. You undertake marine surveys and data collecting after training, and are offered scuba diving training. The data gathered by volunteers is used as the basis of action plans for the conservation and sustainable use of coastal biodiversity. Since 1986, CCC volunteers have helped establish seven new Marine Protected Areas in the Caribbean and Indo-Pacific regions. During the expedition you will have the opportunity to explore the region.

HOW LONG IT WILL LAST

Projects last from two to twelve weeks.

WHERE YOU CAN GO

Honduras and the Philippines. New projects are being planned for Borneo and the Red Sea.

PAYMENT

None.

THE COST TO YOU

The cost varies from about £715 for a two-week stay to £2805 for twelve weeks. This includes full board and lodging and scientific training. Flights are extra, but scuba training is free. If you want scuba training, you need to spend an extra week on the expedition and may pay a supplement for the extra week.

WHO CAN APPLY
You must be between 16 and 70.

WHEN AND HOW TO APPLY
Coral Cay expeditions depart monthly throughout the year. Contact Coral Cay for an application form. If you wish, you have a chance to attend a presentation at venues throughout the UK.

SELECTION PROCESS
None.

PLACEMENT
You choose the expedition you wish to join.

TRAINING
Scuba diving courses are free and you can choose to spend an extra week undertaking a PADI Open Water Diver training course. Boat-handling training can also be given. On arrival, volunteers take part in a series of carefully designed and easy to follow training programmes to equip them with all the knowledge and skills required to work efficiently and safely as a team in remote and challenging environments. Courses range from tropical marine/terrestrial ecology, species identification and survey techniques, to scuba diving (where applicable) and other supporting skills.

SUPPORT FOR PARTICIPANTS
Experienced expedition staff, including an expedition leader, equipment technician, science officer, medical officer and scuba instructor are on hand to ensure that all expedition activities are carried out safely and efficiently.

£-££££

Dorset Expeditionary Society

The Dorset Expeditionary Society is a registered charity which promotes safe adventurous opportunities for young people. Expedition Leaders, who are all volunteers, run up to six overseas expeditions each year which are open to anyone throughout the UK and always take place during the academic summer holidays. Team sizes vary from six to 24, duration from three to five weeks, costs from £500 to £2200. Prior selection and training weekends are held. Activities include mountaineering, jungle survival, kayaking, white water rafting, trekking and mountain biking. The Society has a sponsored training programme, organises social events, produces a regular newsletter, and has a full programme providing opportunities for disadvantaged youth in the UK.

HOW LONG IT WILL LAST
Overseas expeditions last three to five weeks, usually in July/August. Selection and training weekends are timed to coincide with academic holidays.

WHERE YOU CAN GO
Past locations overseas have included the French and Swiss Alps, Alaska, Bolivia, Canada (British Colombia), Dolomites, Ecuador, Iceland, India (Himalayas), Indonesia, Kenya, Mexico, Morocco, Pakistan and Peru.

PAYMENT
None.

THE COST TO YOU
The cost varies, depending on destination and duration. Typical costs are: Alps £500, Ecuador £1900 and Kenya £1000. This includes travel, transport, training, insurance, food and accommodation, etc, and membership of the Society. Leaders are not subsidised and make their own full cash contribution to the expedition.

WHO CAN APPLY
The typical age range is 15 to 21. Previous experience is not required, but you must be fit, healthy and a good team member.

WHEN AND HOW TO APPLY
Apply in September, or soon after, to obtain a place on Selection as places can fill rapidly. However, late applicants are always considered. Apply to the Secretary or via the Internet for an application form.

SELECTION PROCESS
Applicants attend a selection weekend which takes place between September and January, and successful candidates will then be offered a place in the expedition team. Each team member is asked to take on a specific responsibility. Preparatory training days and weekends are then held in the UK.

PLACEMENT
Expedition locations are determined by the Expedition Leaders, who also select their Assistant Leaders. Every year there are one or more 'peer group' expeditions led by Young Leaders (previous expeditioners). You need to be 18+ to join these.

TRAINING
Training days and weekends are held in the UK between December and July, and in most instances also on location as part of the expedition. The Society is also keen to develop Young Leaders and runs a grant scheme for members towards the cost of a wide range of training courses in nationally recognised 'outdoor' qualifications.

SUPPORT FOR PARTICIPANTS
In addition to the experience of overseas travel and the acquisition of skills in survival in the wilderness areas of the world, expedition team members

will also be asked to take responsibility for one crucial element of the expedition, thus developing their own leadership, self-sufficiency and teamworking. The Society provides administrative support, assists with recruitment and provides a database of information. There is also a mentoring programme to support those starting to organise their own venture.

££-£££££ | Encounter

Encounter arranges adventure holidays on overland journeys by expedition trucks to Africa, Asia and South and Central America. Encounter has been in operation for over 33 years and during that time has taken many gap year students on its expeditions. Experiences might include camping, trekking or rafting. Many people take part in Encounter expeditions to start off their travels and to gain confidence in dealing with different cultures and traditions. Most projects involve camping although travellers' hotels are sometimes used where necessary.

HOW LONG IT WILL LAST
Expeditions can last between ten days and thirty-two weeks.

WHERE YOU CAN GO
Asia, Africa, South and Central America.

PAYMENT
None.

THE COST TO YOU
Costs vary according to the length of the expedition and where you go. Land transport, camping and accommodation, meals and entrance fees are included in the price.

WHO CAN APPLY
People of all walks of life and a wide range of countries travel with Encounter. The ratio of men to women is usually even and most people are in their 20s and 30s. You do not need any previous experience of adventure travel.

WHEN AND HOW TO APPLY
Contact Encounter for a brochure and booking details.

SELECTION
None.

PLACEMENT
You apply for the expedition you want to join.

TRAINING
Everyone must be a cooperative member of the team and you will learn how to become part of the expedition as you go along.

SUPPORT FOR PARTICIPANTS
Project leaders are highly trained and dependable in a crisis.

£+ Exodus

Exodus specialises in small-group adventure holidays worldwide across four different programmes: Walking, Biking, Discovery and Overland Expeditions. The Overland Expeditions programme, in which participants travel by truck, is probably most applicable to gap year students. Most of the tours are off the beaten track and everyone contributes to route planning, shopping, cooking and camp chores.

HOW LONG IT WILL LAST
Expeditions last from one week to thirty weeks, depending on the trip.

WHERE YOU CAN GO
Overland tours go to Africa, Asia or South America.

PAYMENT
None.

THE COST TO YOU
Costs start at about £150 per week. This includes transport by expedition truck, services of leaders, ferry fares, road tolls and taxes, use of communal equipment, camping fees (except South America), insurance, entry fees to game parks, and use of standard equipment. Flights and a food kitty are extra.

WHO CAN APPLY
The recommended age is between 18 and 45, but most travellers are 19–35. On longer expeditions to Africa there is a strict age limit of 18 to 40.

WHEN AND HOW TO APPLY
Contact Exodus for their brochures and then ask for the detailed dossiers on the trips you are interested in.

PLACEMENT
You apply for the expedition you are interested in.

TRAINING
Leaders encourage everyone to get the most from an expedition throughout.

SUPPORT FOR PARTICIPANTS
Two leaders accompany almost all expeditions. Passengers are consulted about many decisions during a trip, but the leaders have the last word. Leaders undergo training in the UK and on the road.

Expedition Advisory Centre (Royal Geographical Society)

The RGS does not itself help individuals join expeditions, but gives advice and help to expedition organisers through the Expedition Advisory Centre. It produces many useful publications for potential volunteers and keeps lists of planned expeditions, but cannot place individuals on these.

Anyone between the ages of 16 and 25 may apply for Associate Fellowship of the RGS and can enjoy use of the excellent library, map room, over 3000 indexed expedition reports, receipt of the *Geographical Magazine*, academic journals and newsletters, and a chance to meet other geographers, travellers and explorers at the many lectures, meetings and receptions. Applications forms can be obtained from the Fellowship Secretary.

£££££ Frontier

Frontier is a tropical conservation research and development NGO (non-governmental organisation) that runs expeditions to Tanzania, Madagascar, Vietnam and Mozambique. You have the opportunity to work alongside professional science staff as a research assistant carrying out biodiversity survey and socio-economic research in remote locations. Projects available include marine/diving projects, savannah wildlife projects and tropical forest and rainforest projects.

HOW LONG IT WILL LAST
Each project lasts ten weeks.

WHERE YOU CAN GO
Tanzania, Madagascar, Mozambique or Vietnam.

PAYMENT
None.

THE COST TO YOU
For UK volunteers the cost of a 10-week expedition is £2450 or, for two 10-week expeditions back to back, £3700. This covers accommodation and living costs, project equipment, comprehensive science-training, staff costs, a briefing weekend in the UK, fund-raising advice, full travel and medical documentation and UK and in-country administration.

WHO CAN APPLY
You need to have an interest in habitat and wildlife protection. The key personal qualities that Frontier looks for are resourcefulness, fitness, imagination, flexibility, a willingness to learn and team-working skills. You

do not need a science background, as Frontier staff provide all necessary training. There is no upper age limit, but participants are usually between 17 and 30 years old.

WHEN AND HOW TO APPLY
Information packs (which include an application form) can be requested from the Frontier office or application forms can be downloaded from the Internet.

SELECTION PROCESS
After assessment from application forms, suitable candidates are invited to an interview and briefing session at the Frontier office.

PLACEMENT
Once selected, you choose where and when you go. Changing expeditions is not a problem, provided you give sufficient notice and enough places are available.

TRAINING
You will receive intensive training for the first three to four weeks of your expedition. The skills are specific to each project habitat (marine, forests, etc); all involving a comprehensive suite of ecological survey methods. A series of lectures is given, combined with hands-on practical training. All teaching is by experienced and professional staff. The staff are all paid full-time employees of Frontier who work on their projects from one to four years. Some of the junior staff are also working on individual Open University research PhD degrees, supervised by the more senior staff members. All volunteers, whatever their background, can gain a level 3 BTEC qualification in Tropical Habitat Conservation simply by taking part in the expedition.

SUPPORT FOR PARTICIPANTS
Frontier provides comprehensive fund-raising, medical, travel, equipment and project information and a briefing weekend before you depart; arranges discounted return flights; organises visas; and provides comprehensive survey technique, species identification and language training and team-building. A Volunteer Coordinator is available for advice on all aspects of the expedition and there are full-time permanent logistics and science field staff who work with volunteers. There is a field office, with full communication facilities, located in the relevant country capital or main city.

££££–£££££ | Jagged Globe

This organisation provides opportunities for gap year students to join one of a number of adventurous expeditions, which are aimed specifically at groups of younger people (there is also an extensive brochure of expeditions for the more experienced mountaineer). The programme of mountaineering expeditions requires little or no past climbing experience. Expeditions usually combine any climbing and trekking with both cultural and educational activities.

HOW LONG IT WILL LAST
Expeditions for the young, aspirant mountaineer typically last between two and three weeks.

WHERE YOU CAN GO
Jagged Globe runs group expeditions to all the major mountain ranges around the world, including trips to the Nepalese Himalayas, South America, Africa, Caucasus, Ladakh, Asia and the Pamirs.

PAYMENT
None.

THE COST TO YOU
This depends on the final choice of destination and mountaineering objective. Typically the cost of group expeditions ranges from £1400 and £2250, and includes the cost of flights, accommodation, food and everything else except visa fees, bar bills and travel insurance. Specialist equipment such as boots, sleeping bags, crampons, harnesses, etc, can be hired.

WHO CAN APPLY
Any gap year student can apply. However, it is preferable to get together with some friends and arrange a group expedition, perhaps with the help of your school or college. Group expeditions reduce the cost of the overall trip.

WHEN AND HOW TO APPLY
Contact the organisation direct for details of their school and youth group expeditions programme. Group bookings are usually made through a school or youth group contact, and need to be made well in advance of the expedition to ensure adequate preparation.

SELECTION PROCESS
There is none.

PLACEMENT
None.

TRAINING
All group expeditions undertake pre-expedition training courses. The company also runs introductory snow, ice and Alpine courses for those who wish to improve their winter skills.

SUPPORT FOR PARTICIPANTS
All expedition leaders are qualified, professional mountaineers, and members of the Association of Mountaineering Instructors (AMI) or British Mountain Guides (BMG). Office staff are also active mountaineers or leaders. The company arranges everything.

££–££££

The Tall Ships Experience – Sail Training Association (STA)

Although this is a short-term opportunity, it is included here because it is one of the more unusual and you might like to include it as part of your year off. Two Tall Ships – *Sir Winston Churchill* and *STA Stavros S. Niarchos* – provide adventure voyages. Crews consist of 38 young people from different backgrounds, creeds and nationalities. The ships set sail from various ports around the UK and sail up to 1000 miles, visiting two or three Northern Continental ports. The voyage is a 24-hour-a-day experience, but there is time to relax. The ships also take part in the annual Cutty Sark Tall Ships Race.

HOW LONG IT WILL LAST
The voyages usually last from one to two weeks.

WHERE YOU CAN GO
Most of the youth voyages go to Europe, but there are also winter voyages to the Canaries which cater for an older age range.

PAYMENT
None.

THE COST TO YOU
The cost of voyages varies from about £309 to £1529, depending on the type of voyage and destination. The STA may be able to help with a grant, depending on your circumstances.

WHO CAN APPLY
The youth voyages are for people aged 16–24, but there are voyages which include people aged 18–69. There are no special skills or experience required.

WHEN AND HOW TO APPLY
Contact the Sail Training Association and ask for the Tall Ships Experience brochure.

SELECTION PROCESS
A simple Selection process is applied to ensure that every voyage has a balanced mix of people in the crew. To achieve this the TSE looks at the age range, balance of young men and women on mixed voyages, and the number of people with special needs.

PLACEMENT
You apply for the voyage you want to join.

TRAINING
You will get talks on the workings of the ship and seamanship. The per-

manent crew can offer expert tuition and guidance. Instruction for the RYA Competent Crew Certificate is available.

SUPPORT FOR PARTICIPANTS
The ships have a permanent crew of 14 to give advice. There are thorough safety precautions. You must wear a safety harness at all times when you are on watch.

£££££ | Trekforce Expeditions

Trekforce is the expeditionary arm of the International Scientific Support Trust, a UK-registered charity. They offer you a once in a lifetime opportunity to play your part in international conservation. Expedition projects in Belize and SE Asia concentrate on the endangered rainforest and wildlife, including working with orang-utan rehabilitation in Borneo. Projects in Kenya involve working on community projects on behalf of the Maasi tribespeople.

HOW LONG IT WILL LAST
Placements last from eight weeks for an expedition or five months for longer placements in Central America. This involves an expedition, a month of one-to-one Spanish language training in Guatemala and then eight weeks teaching in a Belizean village.

WHERE YOU CAN GO
Expeditions run in Belize, SE Asia and Kenya.

PAYMENT
None.

THE COST TO YOU
You will need to raise £2350 for eight-week expeditions or £3500 for a five-month programme. Costs include food, transport, accommodation, project costs, training and insurance. International flight is not included. Friendly advice and support are given throughout the fundraising process and some sponsored events are organised by Trekforce.

WHO CAN APPLY
The minimum age is 17, although you may attend an introduction day at 15.

WHEN AND HOW TO APPLY
You can apply at any time of year. Volunteers first attend an introduction day (or interview in the office) and then a briefing day shortly before departure. It is never too early to apply but most people leave at least a year in which to raise the money.

SELECTION PROCESS
Trekforce work on the principle of 'self-selection'. Volunteers should be relatively fit, prepared to work hard, with few home comforts, and work

well as part of a team. They will be in a position to offer you a place after the introduction day/interview.

PLACEMENT
Apply for the expedition you want to go on.

TRAINING
An in-country training/acclimatisation phase starts each expedition and preparation before departure.

SUPPORT FOR PARTICIPANTS
You work as part of a group under the guidance of expedition staff. There are full-time staff in all the countries visited. Full support is provided from the UK office before, during and after the expedition, and ex-trekkers in your area can be contacted for further advice and help.

£££–££££ | The Wilderness Trust

The Wilderness Trust encourages young people to go on wilderness trails with the Wilderness Leadership School in South Africa. The trails give you the chance to gain an insight into the nature of wilderness and the impact of humans on the environment. Journeys are made on foot. You can choose to apply as an individual or as a group. If you apply on your own you will join a group of a maximum of eight people (minimum six people).

HOW LONG IT WILL LAST
Wilderness trails last five, ten or fifteen days with the Wilderness Leadership School.

WHERE YOU CAN GO
Wilderness trails in Natal (Umfolozi Game Reserve, St Lucia Wetlands Park and the Drakensberg mountains) in South Africa.

PAYMENT
None.

THE COST TO YOU
Membership of the Trust costs £10 for students (£20 for other individuals). As an example of prices, a nine-day trail (13-day package ex-UK) to South Africa could cost about £1600, including flights. But prices vary according to the length of the trail and which country you go to. All equipment is provided.

WHO CAN APPLY
You must be over 16.

WHEN AND HOW TO APPLY
Apply at any time through the Wilderness Leadership School and mention contact through the Wilderness Trust

SELECTION PROCESS
None.

TRAINING
None.

SUPPORT FOR PARTICIPANTS
Trail leaders are highly experienced and knowledgeable about the wild, and sensitive to your needs.

SEE ALSO:

Quest Overseas, *page 27*;

Raleigh International, *page 28*;

World Challenge Expeditions, *page 32*

NOW IT'S OVER . . . .

NOW IT'S OVER . . . .

When you arrive home after your year out you will feel tired, excited, and different. It may take time for you to adjust to getting back to your usual routine. If your experience has been a happy one, you will soon settle and be ready for work or college. If you have not enjoyed it so much, you might need a while to adjust and reassess. Whatever your gap year is like, you will probably feel deflated after all the effort and change.

Try to allow yourself time to readjust. Ideally you should aim to arrive home *at least* a week before you start at university or work, in order to have time to make arrangements to begin your next year and to allow for time to room-hunt.

Preparing for the next step

Your immediate tasks should be to make sure that the arrangements for the coming year are still in place and to deal with any last-minute details.

First, open your mail to see whether there is anything you should respond to concerning the next year. If, as advised in chapter 2, you gave one of your parents permission to open your official-looking mail, most things will have been dealt with. They will have either responded on your behalf or contacted you during the gap year so that you could reply. However, there may be last minute-mail you need to deal with, so be methodical.

You then need to check and deal with the following:

▶ details of arrival at college (or work)
▶ accommodation arrangements

▶ registration details

▶ travel arrangements

▶ packing.

If anything concerning your university or college place is unclear, phone them immediately.

If you cannot get a lift to college, book your coach or train journey as soon as possible. Get your packing done too. If you are short of time, pack only the essentials and ask for other things to be brought or sent to you later in the term. You *can* survive without your CD-player, guitar, TV or football for a week or two, for example!

Confirm with the university or college that offered you the place that they are expecting you, and find out when and where to arrive and when to pay hall fees, sign on for the course, etc. If you have a place in hall there will be no problem, but if you are going to be staying in rented accommodation you will need to make arrangements as soon as possible. If you have left it too late, contact the student union housing officer immediately. If there is nothing available you will have to stay in bed and breakfast accommodation until you can find someone to share with or find a room. The important thing is to register and get to your lectures. Once that is done you can set about room hunting.

You should already have contacted your local authority about your fees and arranging your student loan for your first year at university. Phone them as soon as you get back to make sure that the forms have been processed. If there is any problem, make the necessary arrangements immediately and contact your university or college to explain why there is a delay. If necessary, you may have to arrange a loan from your parents or the bank until the money arrives so as not to jeopardise your place.

If you are going to work, a similar action applies. Contact your employer or personnel manager immediately to confirm when they expect you to arrive and who you should see first. If you will be working in another part of the country, ask if they can arrange temporary digs for you until you get settled. Otherwise again find a bed and breakfast through the tourist information office when you arrive and start looking for a room or flat immediately. Ask your new colleagues if they know of anyone who wants a flatmate or knows of a room to let.

Check with your bank manager whether you need to change branches or standing orders. Usually this is not necessary. If you are setting up a new bank account for college, there are usually campus branches you can make arrangements with.

Dealing with the 'gap year feeling'

If you feel a bit 'let down' to start with after your year out, the new experiences you face with a new course or job should soon dispel it. If, however, the feeling does not disappear, there are some practical ways to deal with it.

After a particularly exciting and different gap year, many people find it hard to settle back into their normal routine. Their gap year changed their ideas about what life should be like so much that they want to live as they did on their gap year. Only for a very few people does this kind of dream turn into reality.

If your year out was arranged by an organisation that arranges reunions for its gap year students, do go. It will encourage you to exchange feelings and views with other people who have been through a similar experience. If you still feel deflated once you start university or work, there are worthwhile things that you can do to bring back some of the excitement of your gap year.

If you spent your year out doing voluntary work, ask for information about local voluntary groups at your university or college or through your local library. You could also start a SCA (Student Community Action) group at your university or college (see page 76 under SCADU). By doing so, you will find the same feeling of friendship and will be doing something to help the local community.

If you did voluntary work overseas, consider joining Returned Volunteer Action (RVA). This is a small organisation that provides useful publications and a regular newsletter. It can put you in touch with other returned volunteers who have been in the same country as you. Involvement with RVA can help you make the most of your experience and put it to good use in your return.

If you miss sports, join the college sports society and aim for a qualification or teaching qualification in it. If you discovered a new interest while you were away, you could pursue it in a college or university society or after work. If you acquired new skills, offer your services to local groups.

Many students miss the excitement of travel and new cultures. Team up with friends and arrange to travel during your first long vacation, to give you something to look forward to. Or find out whether you can take part of your course abroad with the ERASMUS scheme.

Changing course

After your year out, you may realise that the course you are about to do is not the one for you. Give it a try first, in case you are just a bit depressed after your trip. If it quickly becomes clear that you cannot stand the course, then ask to change. This *may* be possible if you apply early in the year and can give your tutors a good reason why. In some exceptional cases it may even be possible to change university. Changing courses, or universities, can be easier where courses run on a modular system.

If you should want to change your university, then you must get not only the agreement of your present and new university but agreement from your local authority. Otherwise you will have the choice of staying on and gritting your teeth, and perhaps doing a postgraduate course in your preferred subject; of leaving and working until you have earned enough to pay for taking a new university course; or leaving and starting work and hoping to return as a mature student. If you do leave, then consider an Open University course. You can do this in your spare time while earning money, but you should not consider it an easy option.

If you have started work and decide that it is not for you, then try asking the personnel department whether you can be transferred to another part of the firm. If that is not possible, stay but look around for another job, apply to college or set out to get extra qualifications. You can get careers information and advice from the careers service, private careers advisers and the careers section in your library.

What have you got out of your gap year?

You will certainly be older and wiser after your year out. You will have coped with many varied experiences, good and bad, on your own. You will have become more tolerant of people as individuals and be more aware of the problems and pleasures people face in life. All this will help you to deal with life in a more considered way.

You will also have gained in other ways, for example:

- maturity
- people skills
- confidence
- specific skills
- new interests
- ability to survive on a budget
- money in the bank (if you worked)
- taste for adventure
- new friends
- travel experience.

The most usual skill that you will have acquired is people skills – the ability to get on with other people, to work as part of a team – and perhaps leadership skills. Even if you spent the time travelling on your own, you will have met new people and negotiated with them for food, lodging, etc. These are valuable skills for your CV because employers nowadays look not only for good qualifications but the ability to communicate.

Maturity and people skills bring confidence. You will have become more aware of your own capabilities ahead.

You may have acquired some specific skills, such as a new language, a driving licence, cooking, word processing or carpentry, or general administration experience. These will not only be of practical use to you but can be of use in employment. Some of these skills will be connected to new interests that you can carry over into your spare time – perhaps you learnt to sail or to draw finds on an archaeological excavation. Don't let these new interests drop. They will make you a more interesting and well-rounded person and may even point the way to a career or lasting hobby.

An important skill you will have acquired is how to survive on a budget. Students have a very limited budget so experience of spending your money wisely and surviving on little will go a long way to making life easier for you at university. You may have saved some money from working for part of your year out. In that case you have a head start at college because you have some extra money to survive on.

If you have acquired a taste for adventure, that is something that you can use to spur you on during your life. Make the most of each new situation and look for the interest in it. Take that adventuresome spirit into your outside interests and vacations. A person who looks forward to challenges gets a lot out of life.

Keep in touch with the new friends you made during the past year. Write to them, visit them or arrange a group reunion. By keeping in touch you not only expand your circle of friends but bring your shared experiences into your new life.

Experience of travel is also a useful thing to have. As a student you will have to travel to and from college and about the country visiting friends, taking vacation jobs or going on holiday. Having had experience of dealing with travel situations, perhaps in remote parts of the world, you will find it easy to cope with the problems. You will also know the cheapest ways of travelling.

Whatever new interests, skills and experiences you may have gained, you may be sure that when you arrive back after your year out, the world will seem a more exciting place.

FURTHER READING

A Year Between, by Walter Linstromberg, The Central Bureau, 1999.
Au-pair and Nanny's Guide To Working Abroad, by Susan Griffith & Sharon Legg, Vacation Work, 1997.
Backpacker's Handbook, by Hugh McManners, Dorling Kindersley, 1995.
Backpacking Round Europe, by Mark Hempshell, How To Books, 1997.
The Official UCAS Guide to University and College Entrance, UCAS, annually.
Cheap Eats Guide To Europe, Ebury Press, 1999.
Cheap Sleep Guide To Europe, HarperCollins, 1996.
Cycle UK!, by Les Lumden, Sigma Press, 1994.
Directory of Grant-making Trusts, Charities Aid Foundation, annually.
Directory of Jobs and Careers Abroad, by Jonathan Packer, Vacation Work, 1997.
The Directory of Summer Jobs Abroad, edited by David Woodworth, Vacation Work, annually.
Directory of Summer Jobs in Britain, edited by David Woodworth, Vacation Work, annually.
Distance and Supported Open learning Directory, Open University, 1999.
Doing Voluntary Work Abroad, by Michael Hempshell, How To Books, 1997.
Essential Safety Awareness for Women, by Julie Benjamin, Boatswain Press, 1994.
Floodlight, annually (c/o ALA, 36 Old Queen Street, London SW1H 9JF. Tel: 020 7222 0193. Fax: 020 7976 7434).
Fundraising to Join an Expedition, Expedition Advisory Centre.
Gap Year Guidebook 2000/2001, edited by Rosamund McDougall, Peridot Press, 1999.
Go for it!, edited by Martyn Lewis, Lennard Publishing, 1996.

Home from Home, Central Bureau for Educational Visits and Exchanges, 1994.

How To Find Temporary Work Abroad, by Nick Vandome, How To Books, 1994.

How To get A Job Abroad, by Roger Jones, How To Books, 1996.

How To Study Abroad, by Teresa Tinsley, How To Books, 1995.

The International Directory of Voluntary Work, edited by Victoria Pybus, Vacation Work, 1997.

International Youth Hostels Handbook, YHA.

Joining an Expedition, edited by Shane Winser, Expedition Advisory Centre, 1997.

Kibbutz Volunteer, edited by Victoria Pybus, Vacation Work, 2000.

The Lady, 39–40 Bedford Street, Strand, London WC2E 9ER. Tel: 020 7379 4717. Fax: 020 7497 2137 (weekly).

Live and Work in Germany, by Ian Collier, Vacation Work, 1998.

More Women Travel, edited by Natania Jansz and Miranda Davies, Rough Guides, 1995. The earlier editions are worth reading too: *Half the Earth* and *Women Travel.*

Nothing Ventured: *Disabled People Travel the World*, edited by Alison Walsh, Rough Guides, 1992.

Planning Your Gap Year, by Mark Hempshall, How To Books, 1998.

Sources of Information for Independent and Overland Travellers, edited by Shane Winser, Expedition Advisory Centre, 1993.

Spending A Year Abroad, by Nick Vandome, How To Books, 1999.

Study Abroad 2000-2001, UNESCO, 1999.

Studying in Europe, Careers in Europe, 1995.

Summer Jobs USA, edited by David Woodworth, Vacation Work, annually.

Taking A Year Off, by Val Butcher, Trotman, 1997.

Taking A Gap Year, by Susan Griffith, Vacation Work, 1999.

Teaching English Abroad, Vacation Work, 1994.

Teenager's Vacation Guide To Work, Study & Adventure, by Victoria Pybus, Vacation Work, 1991.

Time to Learn, NIACE (21 de Montfort Street, Leicester LE1 7GE. Tel: 0116 255 1451. Fax: 0116 285 4514, bi-annually, January and August).

The Traveller's Handbook, by Miranda Haines, Sarah Thoroughgood & Michael Palin, WEXAS, 1997.

Traveller's Health: How To Stay Healthy Abroad, How To Books, 1997.

The Traveller's Good Health Guide, by Ted Lancaster, Sheldon Press, 1999.

Tropical Traveller, by John Hatt, Penguin, 1993.

Venture Fund Raising Schemes (free), Raleigh International.

Volunteer Work, edited by Thom Sewell, The Central Bureau, 1995.

Work Your Way Around the World, edited by Susan Griffith, Vacation Work, 1999.

Working Holidays Abroad, by Mark Hempshell, How To Books, 1999.

Working Holidays, The Central Bureau, annually.

Working in Ski Resorts: Europe and North America, Vacation Work, 1997.

Working in the European Community, by A. J. Raban, Hobsons, 1991.

Working in Tourism – the UK, Europe and Beyond, by Verite Reily Collins, Vacation Work, 1998.
Worldwide Volunteering For Young People, How To Books, 1998.
Year Off Handbook, by Roger Jackson, Sabre Publishing, 1997.

This is only a selection of the many useful books available. *How To Books, The Rough Guide To . . .*, and *The Lonely Planet* series of books have many useful and interesting books for travellers. Also look out for other books by publishers in this list. There are also many foreign language dictionaries and phrase books as well as language courses in books and on audio and video tapes – the *Teach Yourself* series (Hodder & Stoughton) covers many of the more unusual languages. Your local library should have a good selection.

Both *Lonely Planet* and *Rough Guides* provide free online newsletters. Read them on www.lonelyplanet.co.uk and www.roughguides.co.uk

Don't forget that many of these books can be bought from internet bookshops such as Amazon at www.amazon.co.uk

See the Vacation Work website at www.vacationwork.co.uk for a complete list of their books.

SOME USEFUL WEBSITES

Association of British Travel Agents (ABTA): www.abtanet.com (for details of your local office)

Backpackers Club, The: www.catan.demon.co.uk/backpack/index.htm

British Airways Travel Clinics: www.british-airways.com/travelqa/fyi/health/health.shtml

British Council, The: www.britishcouncil.org

British Schools Exploring Society: www.bses-expeditions.org.uk

Council on International Educational Exchange (CIEE): www.ciee.org

Department of the Environment, Transport and the Regions: www.detr.gov.uk (for useful e-mail addresses)

Department of Health: www.doh.gov.uk

Department of Social Security: www.dss.gov.uk

English Speaking Union, The (ESU): www.esu.org.uk

Expedition Advisory Centre: www.rgs.org

Foreign & Commonwealth Office, Travel Advice Unit: www.fco.gov.uk/travel

International Student Travel Confederation: www.istc.org

Independent Schools Information Service: www.isis.org.uk

London Transport (Travel Information): www.londontransport.co.uk

Lonely Planet: www.lonelyplanet.co.uk (for free newsletter)

MASTA (Medical Advisory Service for Travellers Abroad: www.masta.org

National Centre for Volunteering: www.volunteering.org.uk

NHS Direct: www.nhsdirect.nhs.uk

National Union of Students (NUS): www.nus.org.uk

Rough Guides: www.roughguides.co.uk (for free newsletter)

UCAS (Universities and Colleges Admissions Service): www.ucas.ac.uk

Year Out Group, The: www.yearoutgroup.org

Youth Exchange Centre, The British Council: www.youthorg.uk/yec

Youth Hostels Association (England and Wales): www.yha.org.uk

39   **Accueil Familial des Jeunes Etrangers**, 23 rue du Cherche Midi, 75006 Paris, France. Tel: 00 33 1 42 22 50 34. Fax: 00 33 1 45 44 60 48. Internet: www.unse.org/organismes/AFJEf.html

23   **Africa & Asia Venture**, 10 Market Place, Devizes, Wiltshire SN10 1HT. Tel: 01380 729009. Fax: 01380 720060. E-mail: av@ aventure.co.uk Internet: www.aventure.co.uk

85   **African Conservation Experience,** PO Box 58, Teignmouth, Devon TQ14 8XW. Tel/fax: 01626 879700. E-mail: info@ afconservex.com Internet: www.afconservex.com

86   **AFS International Youth Development,** Leeming House, Vicar Lane, Leeds LS2 7JF. Tel: 0113 242 6136. Fax: 0113 243 0631. E-mail: info-unitedkingdom@afs.org Internet: www.afsuk.org

41   **AgriVenture**, YFC Centre, NAC, Stoneleigh Park, Kenilworth, Warwickshire CV8 2LG. Tel: FREEPHONE 0800 783 2186. Tel: 02476 696578. Fax: 02476 696684. E-mail: uk@agriventure. com Internet: www.agriventure.com

153   **American Scandinavian Student Exchange (ASSE)**, PO Box 20, Harwich, Essex CO12 4DQ. Tel: 01255 506347. Fax: 01255 240952.

122,   **Archaeology Abroad**, 31–4 Gordon Square, London WC1H OPY4.
131   Tel: 020 7383 2572. E-mail: arch.abroad@ucl.ac.uk Internet: www.britarch.ac.uk/archabroad/guidance.html

147   **Army – Gap Year Commission (GYC)**, FREEPOST, The Army, CV37 9BR. Tel: 08457 300 111. Internet: www.army.mod.uk

154   **Art History Abroad**, Prioryfield House, 20 Canon Street, Taunton, Somerset TA1 1SW. Tel: 01823 323363. Fax: 01823 271072. E-mail: arthistoryabroad@ukbusiness.com Internet: www.ukbusiness.com/ arthistoryabroad

141   **Arvon Foundation, The**, Totleigh Barton, Sheepwash, Beaworthy,

Devon EX21 5NS. Tel: 01409 231338. Fax: 01409 231144 E-mail: t-barton@arvonfoundation.org ; Lumb Bank, Heptonstall, Hebden Bridge, West Yorkshire HX7 6DF. Tel/Fax: 01422 843714 E-mail: l-bank@arvonfoundation.org ; Moniak Mhor, Teavarran, Kiltarlity, Beauly, Inverness-shire IV4 7HT. Tel: 01463 741675. Fax: 01463 741733 E-mail: m-mhor@arvonfoundation.org

131 **Association of British Travel Agents (ABTA)**, 68–71 Newman Street, London W1 4AH. Tel: 020 7637 2444. Fax: 020 7637 0173. E-mail: information@abta.co.uk Internet: www.abtanet.com (check the website for details of your local office).

42 **Athenian Nanny Agency, The,** PO Box 51181, Kifissia 145.10, Athens, Greece. Tel/Fax: 00 301 808 1005. E-mail: mskiniti@groovy.gr

40 **Au-Pair USA**, 161 Sixth Avenue, 13th floor, New York, NY 10013. Tel: 001 212 924 0446. Fax: 001 212 924 0575. Internet: http://interexchange.org/aupair.htm

88 **Australian Trust for Conservation Volunteers (ATCV),** PO Box 423, BALLARAT, Victoria, 3353, Australia. Tel: 00 61 3 5333 1483. Fax: 00 61 3 5333 2166. E-mail: info@atcv.com.au Internet: www.atcv.com.au

132 **Austravel** *London*: Austravel's Great Escape, The Basement, 152 Brompton Road, London SW3 1HX. Tel: 020 7584 0202; 17 Blomfield Street, London EC2M 7AJ. Tel: 020 7588 1516; 50–51 Conduit Street, London W1R 9FB. Tel: 020 7734 7755; *Bristol:* 45 Colston Street, Bristol BS1 5AX. Tel: 0117 927 7425; *Bournemouth:* 107 Old Christchurch Road, Bournemouth BH1 1EP. Tel: 01202 311488; *Leeds:* 16–18 County Arcade, Victoria Quarter, Leeds LS1 6BN. Tel: 0113 244 8880; *Manchester:* 3 Barton Arcade, Deansgate, Manchester M3 2BB. Tel: 0161 832 2445; *Edinburgh*: 33 George Street, Edinburgh EH2 2HN. Tel: 0131 226 1000; *Birmingham*: 12 The Minories, Temple Court, Birmingham B4 6AF. Tel: 0121 200 1116. Internet: www.austravel.net

43 **Avalon Au-Pairs,** 7 Highway, Edgcumbe Park, Crowthorne, Berks RG45 6HE. Tel/Fax: 01344 778246. E-mail: aupair.surrey@mcmail.com

Backpackers Club, The, Internet: www.catan.demon.co.uk/backpack/index.htm

89 **Baptist Missionary Society,** PO Box 49, Didcot, Oxon OX11 8BR. Tel: 01235 517700. E-mail: actionteams@bms.org.uk Internet: www.bms.org.uk

4 **Benefits Agency**, Quarry House, Quarry Hill, Leeds LS2 7UA. Tel: 0113 232 4000. (ask at your local office for useful leaflets).

140 **Birkbeck College**, University of London, Malet Street, London WC1E 7HU. Tel: 020 7631 6000. Fax: 020 7631 6270. Internet: www.bbk.ac.uk

4 **Board of Inland Revenue,** Somerset House, Strand, London WC2R 1LB. Tel: 020 7438 6622. Internet: www.inlandrevenue.gov.uk

142 **BOSS (British Offshore Sailing School)**, Hamble Point Marina, School Lane, Hamble, Hampshire SO31 4NB. Tel: 023 8045 7733.

Fax: 023 8045 6744. E-mail: enquiry@boss-sail.co.uk Internet: www.boss-sail.co.uk

165 **Brathay Exploration Group,** Brathay Hall, Ambleside, Cumbria LA22 0HP. Tel: 015394 33942.

Brethren Volunteer Service (BVS), World Ministries Commission, Church of the Brethren General Board, 1451 Dundee Avenue, Elgin, Illinois 60120, USA. Tel: 001 800 323 8039 or 001 847 742 5100. Fax: 001 847 742 6103.

17, **British Airways Travel Clinics.** Tel: 01276 685040 Internet: www.
18 british-airways.com/travelqa/fyi/health/health.shtml (for locations of BA travel clinics).

140 **British Council, The,** 10 Spring Gardens, London SW1A 2BN. *General enquiries* Tel: 0161 957 7755. Fax: 0161 957 7762. E-mail: general.enquiries@britcoun.org *Education enquiries* Tel: 020 7389 4383. Fax: 020 7389 4292. E-mail: education.enquiries@britcoun.org Internet: www.britishcouncil.org

155 **British Institute of Florence, The,** Language Centre, Piazza Strozzi 2, 50123 Florence, Italy. Tel: 00 39 55 26778200. Fax: 00 39 55287071. E-mail: info@britishinstitute.it Internet: www.britishinstitute.it

166 **British Schools Exploring Society,** Royal Geographical Society, 1 Kensington Gore, London SW7 2AR. Tel: 020 7591 3141. Fax: 020 7591 3140. E-mail: bses@rgs.org Internet: www.bses-expeditions.org.uk

120 **British Tourist Authority,** Thames Tower, Blacks Road, London W6 9EI. Tel: 020 8846 9000. Internet: www.visitbritain.com *Ireland*: 18–19 College Green, Dublin 2, Ireland. Tel: 00 353 1 670 8000. Fax: 00 353 1 670 8244.

121 **BTCV (British Trust for Conservation Volunteers),** 36 St Mary's Street, Wallingford, Oxon OX10 0EU. Tel: 01491 839766. Fax: 01491 839646. E-mail:information@btcv.org.uk Internet: www.btcv.org

44 **BUNAC,** Working Adventures Worldwide, Membership Department, BUNAC, 16 Bowling Green Lane, London EC1R 0QH. Tel: 020 7251 3472. Fax: 020 7251 0215. E-mail: enquiries@bunac.org.uk Internet: www.bunac.org

Bus Eireann, Internet: www.buseireann.ie

35, **Camp America,** 37a Queen's Gate, London SW7 5HR. Tel: 020
45 7581 7373. E-mail: brochure@campamerica.co.uk Internet: www.campamerica.co.uk

61 **Camphill Communities.** These are the ones mentioned in the text. Any of the communities should be able to provide you with a com-
62 plete list or check the country website. *Camphill Community Beannachar*, Beacnnachar, South Deeside Road, Banchory-Devenick, Aberdeen AB12 5YL. Tel/Fax: 01224 869250 E-mail: beannachar@talk21.com; *Camphill Rudolph Steiner Schools*,
62 Central Office, Murtle House, Bieldside, Aberdeen AB15 9EP. Tel: 01224 867935. Fax: 01224 868420 E-mail:office@crss.org.uk; *Camphill Special School–Beaver Run*, 1784

Fairview Road, Glenmoore, Pennsylvania 19343, USA. Tel: 001 610 469

90   9236. Fax: 001 610 469 9758; *Camphill Village USA Inc*, Copake, NY 12516, USA. Tel: 001 518 329 4851. Fax: 001 518

62   329 0377; *Mourne Grange Camphill Village Community*, 169 Newry Road, Kilkeel, Co Down BT34 4EX. Tel: 02830 760 128. Fax: 02830 765 372. E-mail: 100653.2371@compuserve.com;

63   *Pennine Camphill Community*, Boyne Hill, Chapelthorpe, Wakefield, West Yorkshire WF4 3JH. Tel: 01924 255281. Fax: 01924 240257. E-mail: office@pennine.org Internet: www.

110   pennine.org.uk; *Staffansgården*, Furugatan 1, Box 66, 820 60 Delsbo, Sweden. Tel: 0046 0653 168 50. Fax: 0046 0653 109 68. Internet (by country): *England, Northern Ireland* www. camphill.org.uk; *Republic of Ireland* www.camphill.ie; *Scotland* www.camphillscotland.org.uk

63   **Careforce,** 35 Elm Road, New Malden, Surrey KT3 3HB. Tel: 020 8942 3331. E-mail: enquiry@careforce.co.uk Internet: www. careforce. co.uk www.camphillscotland.org.uk

121   **Cathedral Camps,** 16 Glebe Avenue, Flitwick, Bedfordshire MK45 1HS. Tel: 01525 716237. E-mail:info@cathedralcamps.org.uk Internet: www.cathedralcamps.org.uk

133   **Central Bureau, The**, 10 Spring Gardens, London SW1A 2BN. Tel: 020 7389 4886. E-mail: cblon.information@britishcouncil.org

46   **Challenge Educational Services**, 101 Lorna Road, Hove, East Sussex BN3 3EL. Tel: 01273 220261. Fax: 01273 220376. E-mail: enquiries@challengeuk.com Internet: www.challengeuk.com

     Chantiers Archéologiques pour Bénévoles, Direction du Patrimoine, Sous-Direction de l'Archéologie, Documentation, 4 rue d'Aboukir, 75002 PARIS, France.

47   **Childcare International Ltd**, Trafalgar House, Grenville Place, London NW7 3SA. Tel: 020 8906 3116. Fax: 020 8906 3461. E-mail: office@childint.co.uk Internet: www.childint.co.uk

     Christian Service Centre, Holloway Street West, Lower Gornal, West Midlands DYS 2DZ.

82   **Christians Abroad** – see World Service Enquiry

64   **Church Mission Society (CMS)**, Partnership House, 157 Waterloo Road, London SE1 8UU. Tel: 020 7928 8681. Fax: 020 7401 3215. E-mail: kathy.tyson@cms-uk.org Internet: www.cms-uk.org

48   **CIEE: Council on International Educational Exchange**, 52 Poland Street, London W1V 4JQ. Tel: 020 7478 2000. Fax: 020 7734 7322. E-mail: InfoUK@ciee.org Internet: http://www.ciee.org

91   **CMJ (Church's Ministry among Jewish People),** 30c Clarence Road, St Albans, Herts AL1 4JJ. Tel: 01727 833114. Fax: 01727 848312. E-mail: enquiries@cmj.org.uk Internet: www.cmj.org.uk

92   **Concordia (YSV) Ltd,** 20–22 Heversham House, Boundary Road, Hove BN3 4ET. Tel/fax: 01273 422218. Internet: http:// freespace.virginnet.co.uk/ivps.conc/index.htm

65   **Conservation Volunteers Northern Ireland (CVNI),** Angie Davis, Belfast (Volunteer) Information Officer, Beech House, 159 Ravenshill Road, Belfast BT6 0BP. Tel: 028 9064 5169. Fax: 028

9064 4409. E-mail: CVNI@btcv.org.uk.

167 **Coral Cay Conservation,** 154 Clapham Park Road, London SW4 7DE. Tel: 020 7498 6248 (24 hour). Fax: 020 7498 6248. Fax: 020 7498 8447. E-mail: ccc@coralcay.org Internet: www.coralcay.org

66 **Corrymeela Community, The,** The Volunteer Coordinator, 5 Drumaroan Road, Ballycastle, Co. Antrim BT54 6QU. Tel: 012657 62626. Fax: 012657 62770. E-mail: ballycastle@corrymeela.org.uk Internet: www.corrymeela.org.uk

122 **Council for British Archaeology (CBA),** Bowes Morrell House, 111 Walmgate, York YO1 2UA. Tel: 01904 671417. Fax: 01904 671384. E-mail: archaeology@csi.com Internet: www.britarch.ac.uk

156 **Council on International Educational Exchange (CIEE),** 52 Poland Street, London W1V 4JQ. Tel: 020 7478 2000. Fax: 020 7734 7322. E-mail: infoUK@councilexchanges.org.uk Internet: www,ciee.org

133 **Council Travel,** 52 Poland Street, London W1V 4JQ. Tel: 020 7478 2000. Fax: 020 7734 7322. E-mail: infoUK@councilexchanges. org.uk

93 **Crusoe,** Crusaders International, 2 Romeland Hill, St Albans, Herts AL3 4ET. Tel: 01727 855422. Fax: 01727 848518. E-mail: crusoe@crusaders.org.uk Internet: www.crusaders.org.uk

67 **CSV (Community Service Volunteers),** 237 Pentonville Road, London N1 9NJ. FREEPHONE: 0800 374991(for information and application pack). Fax: 020 7833 0149. E-mail: volunteer@ csv.org.uk Internet: http://www.csv.org.uk

120 **Cyclists' Touring Club,** Cotterrell House, 69 Meadrow, Godalming, Surrey GU7 3HS. Tel: 01483 417217. Fax: 01483 426994. E-mail: cycling@ctc.org.uk Internet: www.ctc.org.uk

Department for Education and Employment (DFEE), Sanctuary Buildings, Great Smith Street, London SW1P 3BT. Tel: 020 7925 5555. Fax: 01928 794248. E-mail: info@dfee.gov.uk Internet: www.dfee.gov.uk

Department of the Environment, Transport and the Regions Eland House, Bressenden Place, London SW1E 5DU. Tel: 020 7944 3000. Internet: www.detr.gov.uk (for useful e-mail addresses)

Department of Health, Richmond House, 79 Whitehall, London SW1A 2NL. Tel: 020 7210 2000. E-mail: dhmail@doh.gsi.gov.uk Internet: www.doh.gov.uk

Department of Health & Social Services Northern Ireland, Castle Buildings, Stormont, Belfast BT4 3PP. Tel: 028 9052 0000. Fax: 028 9052 0572.

Department of Social Security, Headquarters Correspondence Unit, Room 540, The Adelphi, 1-11 John Adam Street, London WC2N 6HT. Tel: 020 7712 2171. Fax: 020 7712 2386. E-mail: peo@MS41.dss.gsi.gov.uk Internet: www.dss.gov.uk

Directory of Social Change, 24 Stephenson Place, London NW1 2DP. Tel: 020 7209 4949. E-mail: webmaster@d-s-c.demon.co.uk Internet: www.d-s-c.demon.co.uk

168 **Dorset Expeditionary Society,** c/o Budmouth Technology College, Chickerell Road, Weymouth, Dorset DT4 9SY. Tel: 01305

775599.Fax: 01305 766389. E-mail: dorsetexp@wdi.co.uk
Internet: www.dorsetexp.co.uk

Drugs Prevention Advisory Service (DPAS), Room 314, Horseferry House, Dan Ryle street, London SW1P 2AW. Tel: 020 7217 8631. Fax: 020 7217 8230. E-mail: homeofficedpashq@btinternet.com Internet: www.homeoffice.gov.uk/dpas/dpas.htm (Home Office drugs branch).

143 **Duke of Edinburgh's Award, The,** Gulliver House, Madeira Walk, Windsor SL4 1EU. Tel: 01753 727400. Fax: 01753 810666. E-mail: info@theaward.org Internet: www.theaward.org

133 **Earthwatch,** 57 Woodstock Road, Oxford OX2 6HJ. Tel: 01865 311600. Fax: 01865 311383. E-mail: info@uk.earthwatch.org Internet: www.earthwatch.org

68 **Edinburgh Cyrenians,** The Project Manager, 107a Ferry Road, Edinburgh EH6 4ET. Tel/Fax: 0131 555 3707. E-mail: edinburgh.cyrenians@virgin.net

49, **EIL**, 287 Worcester Road, Malvern, Worcestershire WR14 1AB. Tel:
95 01684 562577. Fax: 01684 56212. E-mail: info@eiluk.org Internet: www.eiluk.org

Embassies and Consulates – addresses and phone numbers can be found in *Whitaker's Almanack* which will be in your local reference library.

156 **En Famille Overseas**, The Old Stables, 60b Maltreavers Street, Arundel, West Sussex BN18 9BG. Tel: 01903 883266. Fax: 01903 883582.

170 **Encounter,** 267 Old Brompton Road, London SW5 9JA. Tel: 020 7370 6845. Fax: 020 7244 9737. E-mail: adventure@encounter-overland.co.uk Internet: www.encounter.co.uk

157 **English Speaking Union, The (ESU)**, Dartmouth House, 37 Charles Street, London W1X 8AB. Tel: 020 7493 3328. Fax: 020 7495 6108. E-mail: esu@esu.org Internet: www.esu.org.uk

158 **Euro-Academy Ltd**, 77a George Street, Croydon CR0 1LD. Tel: 020 8686 2363. Fax: 020 8681 8850. E-mail: euroacademy@ btinternet. com Internet: www.euroacademy.co.uk

49 **Eurocamp**, Overseas Recruitment Department, Eurocamp, Hartford Manor, Northwich, Cheshire CW8 1HW Tel: 01565 625522. E-mail: enquiries@eurocamp.co.uk Internet: www.holidaybreak.co.uk recruit/recruitment.html

134 **Eurolines**, Tel: 01582 415841. E-mail: welcome@eurolines.co.uk Internet: www.eurolines.co.uk

159 **European Educational Opportunities Programme**, 60–61 Biggin Street, Dover, Kent CT16 1DD. CT15 7ET. Tel: 01304 211044. Fax: 01304 211130. E-mail: suebugden@eeop.com Internet: www.eeop.com

160 **European Union Youth Orchestra**, 65 Sloane Street, Victoria, London SW1X 9SH. Tel: 020 7235 7671. Fax: 020 7235 7030. E-mail: info@euyo.org.uk Internet: www.euyo.org.uk

171 **Exodus**, 9 Weir Road, London SW12. Tel: 020 8675 5550; 020 8673 0859 (brochures 24-hour answer line). Fax: 020 8673 0779. E-mail: sales@exodustravels.co.uk

172 **Expedition Advisory Centre**, Royal Geographical Society, 1 Kensington Palace Gore, London SW7 2AR. Tel: 020 7591 3030. Fax: 020 7591 3031. E-mail: eac@rgs.org Internet: www.rgs.org

94 **Experience Exchange Programme,** USPG, Partnership House, 157 Waterloo Road, London SE1 8XA. Tel: 020 7928 8681. Fax: 020 7928 2371. E-mail: eep@uspg.org.uk; The Methodist Church, World Church Office, 25 Marylebone Road, London NW1 5JR. Tel: 020 7486 5502. Fax: 020 7467 5227. E-mail: eep@MethodistChurch.org.uk

69 **Ffestiniog Railway,** Harbour Station, Porthmadog, Gwynedd, Wales LL49 9NF. Tel: 01766 512340. Fax: 01766 514715. E-mail: info@festrail.co.uk Internet: www.festrail.co.uk

144 **Field Studies Council,** Head Office, Preston Montford, Shrewsbury, Shropshire SY4 1HW. Tel: 01743 850674. Fax: 01743 850178. E-mail: fsc.headoffice@ukonline.co.uk Internet: www.field-studies-council.org

19 **Foreign & Commonwealth Office,** Travel Advice Unit, Consular Division, Foreign and Commonwealth Office, 1 Palace Street, London SW1 5HE. Tel: 020 7238 4503/4504. Fax: 020 7238 4545. Internet: www.fco.gov.uk/travel

50 **French Encounters**, Patsy Musto, French Encounters, 63 Fordhouse Road, Bromsgrove, Worcestershire B60 2LU. Tel: 01527 873645. Fax: 01527 832794; *Château de la Guerche*, 76490 Caudebec-en-Caux, Seine Maritime, France. Tel: 00 33 2 35 56 97 77; *Domaine des Hellandes*, 76280 Angerville l'Orcher, Seine Maritime, France. Tel: 00 33 2 35 20 59 09.

96 **Friends of Israel Educational Trust,** PO Box 7545, London NW2 2QZ. Tel: 020 7435 6803. Fax: 020 7794 0291. E-mail: foiasg@foiasg.free-online.co.uk

172 **Frontier,** 77 Leonard Street, London EC2A 4QS. Tel: 020 7613 2422. Fax: 020 7613 2992. E-mail: enquiries@frontierprojects.ac.uk Internet: www.frontierprojects.ac.uk

24 **GAP Activity Projects (GAP),** GAP House, 44 Queen's Road, Reading, Berkshire RG1 4BB. Tel: 0118 959 4914. Fax: 0118 957 6634. E-mail: Volunteer@gap.org.uk Internet: www.gap.org.uk

161 **Goethe-Institut**, Sonnenstraße 25, D-80331 München, Germany. Tel: 00 49 089 55 1903 0. Fax: 00 49 089 55 1903 35. E-mail: muenchen@goethe.de Internet: www.goethe.de.

97 **Habitat for Humanity Great Britain,** The Malt House, 11 Parsons Street, Banbury OX16 8LW. Tel: 01295 264240. Fax: 01295 264230. E-mail: HFG_GB@compuserve.com Internet: www.habitat.org

97 **Habitat for Humanity International,** 121 Habitat Street, Americus, GA 31709-3498, USA. Tel: 001 912 924 6935. Fax: 001 912 924 6541.

Health Literature Hotline, Tel: 0800 555 777 (free information and details of books produced by the Department of Health and the Health Education Authority on aspects of health and travel).

98 Health Projects Abroad (HPA), PO Box 24, Bakewell, Derbyshire DE45 1ZW. Tel: 01629 640051. Fax: 01629 640054. E-mail: info@hpauk.org Internet: www.hpauk.org

14 HM Customs & Excise. Internet: www.hmce.gov.uk (for information and contact details of advice centres).

51 Home From Home, Au-pair Agency, Walnut Orchard, Chearsley, Aylesbury, Buckinghamshire HP18 0DA. Tel/fax: 01844 208561.

17 Hospital for Tropical Diseases, 4 St Pancras Way, London NW1 0PE. Tel: 020 7387 4411. Fax back service: 0991 991 992. Travel Clinic Helpline. Tel: 0839 337733 (premium line).

138 Independent Schools Information Service, ISIS Central, Woodstock, Oxon OX7 1YF. Tel: 01993 81306. Fax: 01993 811400. E-mail: central@isis.org.uk Internet: www.isis.org.uk

99 Indian Volunteers for Community Service (IVCS), 12 Eastleigh Avenue, South Harrow, Middlesex HA2 0UF. Tel: 020 8864 4740. Fax: 020 8930 8338. E-mail: endah@dircon.co.uk www.ivcs .dircon.co.uk

140 International House Teacher Training, International House, 106 Picadilly, London W1V 9FL. Tel: 020 7491 2598. Fax: 020 7409 0959. E-mail: info@ihlondon.co.uk Internet: www.international-house-london.ac.uk

100 International Voluntary Service (IVS), *IVS South*, Old Hall, East Bergholt, Colchester CO7 6TQ. Tel: 01206 298215. Fax: 01206 299043 E-mail: ivs@ivsgbsouth.demon.co.uk; *IVS North*, Castlehill House, 21 Otley Road, Leeds LS6 3AA. Tel: 0113 2304600. Fax: 0113 2304610. E-mail: ivs@ivsgbn.demon.co.uk; *IVS Scotland*, 7 Upper Bow, Edinburgh EH1 2JN. Tel: 0131 226 6722. Fax: 0131 226 6723. E-mail: neil@ivsgbscot.demon.co.uk Internet: www.ivsgbn.demon.co. uk

101 International Voluntary Service – Northern Ireland, 122 Great Victoria Street, Belfast BT2 7BG. Tel:1232 238 238147. Fax: 01232 244356. E-mail:ivsni@dnet.co.uk

52 Inter-Séjours, 179 rue de Courcelles, 75017 Paris, France. Tel: 00 33 1 47 63 06 81. Fax: 00 33 1 40 54 89 41. E-mail: intersejours@ europost.org

102 Interserve, 325 Kennington Road, London SE11 4QH. Tel: 020 7735 8227. Fax: 020 7587 5362. E-mail: isewi@isewi.globalnet.co.uk Internet: www.interserve.org/ew

70 Iona Community, Iona Abbey, Isle of Iona, Argyll, PA76 6SN, Scotland. Tel: 01681 700 404. Fax: 01681 700 460. E-mail: ionacomm@iona.org.uk Internet: www.iona.org.uk

71 Ironbridge Gorge Museum, The , The Ironbridge Gorge Museum Trust, Ironbridge,. Telford, Shropshire TF8 7AW. Tel: 01952 433 522. Fax: 01952 432 204. E-mail: info@ironbridge.org.uk Internet: www.ironbridge.org.uk

11 **ISIC**, Internet: www.istc.org (for addresses of local offices issuing ISIC cards).

104 **Jacob's Well Appeal,** 2 Ladygate, Beverley, East Yorks HU17 8BH. Tel: 01482 881162. Fax: 01482 865452. E-mail: 100575.2205@ compuserve.com

173 **Jagged Globe,** The Foundry Studios, 45 Mowbray Street, Sheffield S3 8EN. Tel: 0114 276 3322. Fax: 0114 276 3344. E-mail: expeditions@jagged-globe.co.uk Internet: www.jagged-globe. co.uk

105 **Kibbutz Representatives,** 1a Accommodation Road, Golders Green, London NW11 8ED. Tel: 020 8458 9235. Fax: 020 8455 7930.

106 **Latin Link,** 175 Tower Bridge Road, London SE1 2AB. Tel: 020 7939 9004 (Stride). Tel: 020 7939 9014 (Step). E-mail: Stride.uk@latin link.org or Step.uk@latinlink.org

72 **Leonard Cheshire Foundation, The,** 26–9 Maunsel Street, London SW1P 2QN. Tel: 020 7802 8200. Fax: 020 7802 8250.

152 **Leonardo Da Vinci,** The British Council, 10 Spring Gardens, London SW1A 2BN. Tel: 020 7389 4004. E-mail: leonardo@ britishcouncil.org Internet: www.leonardo.org

152 **LINGUA,** UK Lingua Unit, The Central Bureau, 10 Spring Gardens, London SW1 2BN. Tel: 020 7389 4596. Fax: 020 7389 4426. E-mail: cblon.socrates@britishcouncil.org Internet: www.britcoun. org.uk

73 **London City Mission,** Special Projects Department, 175 Tower Bridge Road, London SE1 2AH. Tel: 020 7407 7585. Fax: 020 7403 6711. E-mail: lcm@btinternet.com Internet: www.lcm.org.uk

120 **London Transport (Travel Information),** 55 Broadway, London SW1H 0BD. Tel: 020 7222 1234 (24-hour enquiries). Tel: 020 7222 1200 (Travelcheck – regularly updated travel news). Internet: www.londontransport.co.uk Teletext: ITV page 164 or BBC page 436.

17 **Malaria Healthline**, Tel: 0891 600 350 (premium line).

17 **MASTA (Medical Advisory Service for Travellers Abroad)**, 24-hour Traveller's Healthline. Tel: 0906 8224100 (premium line). E-mail: masta.sales@dial.pipex.com Internet: www.masta.org

17 **Medicentre,** Tel: 020 7931 9824.

18 **National AIDS Helpline,** Tel: 0800 567123 (free and confidential, 24 hours a day).
   National Drugs Helpline, Tel: 0800 77 66 00 (free and confidential, 24 hours a day).
   National Centre for Volunteering, Tel: 020 7520 8900. Fax: 020 7520 8910. E-mail: Information@thecentre.org.uk Internet: www.volunteering.org.uk

120 **National Express,** Tel: 08705 808080. Internet: www.nationalexpress. co.uk

120 **National Rail Enquries,** Tel: 0345 484950. (see also **Railtrack**)
73,   **National Trust,** PO Box 84, Cirencester, Glos. GL7 1ZP.
123
16   **NHS Direct**, Tel: 0845 4647 (24-hour health helpline). Internet: www.nhsdirect.nhs.uk
135 **North South Travel**, Moulsham Mill Centre, Parkway, Chelmsford, Essex CM2 7PX. Tel: 01245 492882. Fax: 01245 356612. E-mail: brenda@nstravel.demon.co.uk Internet:www.nstravel.demon.co.uk
74   **Northern Ireland Volunteer Development Agency,** Annsgate House, 70–4 Ann Street, Belfast BT1 4EH. Tel: 0232 26100. Fax: 0232 237570.
     NUS, Internet: www.nus.org.uk

107 **Oasis,** Oasis Trust, 115 Southwark Bridge Road, London SE1 0AX. Tel: 020 7450. Fax: 020 7450 9001. E-mail: OasisTrust@ compuserve.com. Internet: http://www.u-net.com/oasis
124 **Ocean Youth Trust**, The Bus Station, South Street, Gosport, Hants PO12 1EP. Tel:023 9252 8421. Fax: 023 9252 2069. *South:* oytweb @davidho.demon.co.uk; *North West*: E-mail:steve@oycnorthwest. freeserve.co.uk; *North East:* oyt.northeast@virgin.net; *Scotland:* 24 Blythswood Square, Glasgow G2 4QS. Tel: 0141 300 551. Fax: 0141 200 5701. E-mail: em-office@oytscotland.org.uk Internet: www.oytscotland.org.uk
75   **Ockenden International,** Mrs Pat Moseley, Personnel Officer, Constitution Hill, Woking, Surrey GU22 7UU. Tel: 01483 772012. Fax: 01483 750774. E-mail: oi@ockenden.org.uk Internet: www.ockenden.org.uk
139 **Open College of the Arts**, Registration Department, FREEPOST, Barnsley, S70 6TU. FREEPHONE: 0800 731 2116. Fax: 01266 730 838. E-mail: open.arts@ukonline.co.uk Internet: www. oca-uk.com
     Open University, **The,** Central Enquiry Service, PO Box 200, Milton Keynes MK7 6YZ. Tel: 01908 653231. Fax: 01908 654806. E-mail: ces-gen@open.ac.uk Internet: www.open.ac.uk
108 **Operation Mobilisation,** The Quinta, Weston Rhyn, Oswestry, Shropshire SY10 7LT. Tel: 01691 773388. Fax: 01691 778378. E-mail: info@uk.om.org Internet: www.pcug.co.uk
     Operation Osprey, RSPB, Grianan, Tulloch, Nethybridge, Invernesshire PH25 3EF. Tel: 01479 831694.
     Opportunities Abroad, World Service Enquiry, 1, Stockwell Green, London SW9 9HP (subscription only – it contains the latest vacancies with aid, development and mission agencies overseas and in the UK).
144 **Outward Bound,** Outward Bound Trust, Watermillock, Nr Penrith, Cumbria CA11 0JL. Tel: 0990 134227. Fax: 017684 86983. E-mail: enquiries@outwardbound-uk.org Internet: www.outward bound-uk.org

11   **Passport Agency, UK,** Tel: 0870 521 0410 (National enquiry line). Clive House, Petty France, London SW1H 9HD; 5th floor, India

Buildings, Water Street, Liverpool L2 0QZ; Olympia House, Upper Dock Street, Newport, Gwent, NP9 1XA; Aragon Court, Northminster Road, Peterborough PE1 1QG; 3 Northgate, 96 Milton Street, Cowcaddens, Glasgow G4 0BT; Hampton House, 47–53 High Street, Belfast BT1 2QS.

53   **PGL Adventure,** Seasonal Personnel Dept., PGL Travel Ltd, Alton Court, Penyard Lane, Ross-On-Wye, Herefordshire HR9 5NR. Tel: 01989 767833. Fax: 01989 768769. E-mail: recruitment@ pgl.co.uk Internet: www.pgl.co.uk/personnel

54   **Pro Filia,** Bureau de Placement, 51 rue de Carouge, 1205 Genève, Switzerland. Tel/fax: 00 41 22 329 84 62.

26   **Project Trust**, The Director, Project Trust, The Hebridean Centre, Isle of Coll, Argyll, PA78 6TE. Tel: 01879 230 444. Fax: 01879 230 357. Internet: www.projecttrust.org.uk

27   **Quest Overseas**, 32 Clapham Mansions, Nightingale Lane, London SW4 9AQ. Tel: 0208 673 3313. Fax: 0208 673 7623. E-mail: emailus@ questoverseas.com Internet: www.questoverseas.com

120   **Railtrack**, Internet: www.railtrack.co.uk (for national timetables).

28   **Raleigh International,** Raleigh House, 27 Parson's Green Lane, London SW6 4HZ. Tel: 020 7371 8585. Fax: 020 7371 5116. E-mail: info@raleigh.org.uk Internet: www.raleigh.org.uk

120   **Ramblers Association,** 1–5 Wandsworth Road, London SW8 2XX. Tel: 020 7339 8500. Fax: 020 7339 8501. E-mail: ramblers@ london.ramblers.org.uk Internet: www.ramblers.org.uk; *Wales:* Ty'r Cerddwyr, High Street, Gresford, Wrexham, Clywd LL12 8PT. Tel: 01798 855148. Fax: 01798 854445. E-mail: cerddwyr@wales.ramblers. org.uk; *Scotland:* Kingfisher House, Auld Mart Business Park, Milnathort, Kinross KY13 9DA. Tel: 01577 861222. Fax: 01577 861333. E-mail: enquiries@scotland. ramblers.org.uk

135   **REMPART,** 1 rue des Guillemites, 75004 Paris, France. Tel: 00 33 1 42 71 96 55. Fax: 00 33 1 42 71 73 00.

55   **Resort America**, 37a Queen's Gate, London SW7 5HR. Tel: 020 7581 7303. E-mail: brochure@resortamerica.co.uk Internet: www.resor tamerica.co.uk

181   **Returned Volunteer Action,** 1 Amwell Street, London EC1R 1TH. Tel: 020 7278 0804. Fax: 020 7278 7019.

29   **Right Hand Trust, The**, Gelligason, Llanfair Caereinion, Powys SY21 9HE. Tel/Fax: 01938 810215. E-mail: righthandtrust@ compuserve.com Internet: http://members.tripod.co.uk/right handtrust

76   **Royal Society for the Protection of Birds (RSPB),** YOC National Volunteers Coordinator, The Lodge, Sandy, Bedfordshire SG19 2DL. Tel: 01767 680551. Fax: 01767 692365.

109   **SAMS (South American Mission Society),** Unit 11, Prospect Business Park, Langston Road, Loughton, Essex IG10 3TZ. Tel/fax: 0208 502 3504. E-mail: SAMSpersonnel@compuserve.com

76 **SCADU (The National Centre for Student Volunteering in the Community)**, Oxford House, Derbyshire Street, London E2 6HG. Tel: 020 7739 4565/0918. Fax: 020 7729 0435. E-mail: scadu@dial.pipex.com Internet: www.scadu.org.uk

30 **Schools Partnership Worldwide (SPW),** 17 Dean's Yard, London SW1P 3BP. Tel: 020 7222 0138. Fax: 020 7233 0008. E-mail: spwuk@gn.apc.org Internet: www.spw.org

Scottish Citylink Services, Buchanan Bus Station, Killermont Street, Glasgow G3 2NP. Tel: 08705 50 50 50. Fax: 0141 332 4488. E-mail: info@citylink.demon.co.uk Internet: www.citylink. co.uk

76 **Scripture Union**, YeS You Scheme, 207–9 Queensway, Bletchley, Bucks MK2 2EB. Tel: 01908 856600. E-mail: missions@ scripture union.org.uk Internet: www.scripture.org.uk

77 **SHAD Wandsworth,** Recruitment Worker, 5 Bedford Hill, London SW12 9ET. Tel: 020 8675 6095. Fax: 020 8673 2118. E-mail: shadwand@aol.com Internet: www.shad.org.uk

78 **Shaftsbury Society, The**, 16 Kingston Road, London SW19 1JZ. Tel: 020 8239 5555.

79 **Simon Community, The,** PO Box 1187, London NW5 4HW. Tel: 020 7485 6639. Fax: 020 7482 6305.

150, **SOCRATES-ERASMUS,** UK SOCRATES-ERASMUS Council,
152, Research & Development Building, The University of Kent, Canter-
181 bury, Kent CT2 7PD. Tel: 01227 762 712. Fax: 01227 762 711. E-mail: erasmus@ukc.ac.uk Internet: http://speke.ukc.ac.uk/erasmus/erasmus

31 **St David's (Africa) Trust**, Beaufort Chambers, Beaufort Street, Crickhowell, Powys, Wales NP8 1AA. Tel/fax: 01873 810665. E-mail: wales@africatrust.gi Internet: www.africatrust.gi

136 **STA Travel,** Telesales: 020 7361 6145 (Europe), 020 7361 6144 (worldwide)., 020 7361 6150 (insurance, overland travel) Internet: www.statravelgroup.co.uk

111 **Sunseed Trust, The,** Tel/fax: 01273 387731. E-mail: stu-max @toff.freeserve.co.uk Internet: www.sunseed.clara.net

125 **Sustrans**, Head Office, 35 King Street, Bristol BS1 4DZ. *Information and sales*: Tel: 0117 929 0888. Fax: 0117 915 0124. E-mail: info@sustrans.org.uk Internet: www.sustrans.org.uk

141, **Taliesin Trust,** Tŷ Newydd, Llanstumdwy, Cricieth, Gwynedd LL52
145 0LW. Tel:01766 522811. Fax: 01766 523095. E-mail: tynewydd @dial. pipex.com

175 **Tall Ships Experience, The,** Sail Training Association, 2a The Hard, Portsmouth, Hampshire PO1 3PT. Tel: 023 9283 2055. Fax: 023 9281 5769. E-mail: tallships@sta.org.uk Internet: www.sta.org.uk

112 **Teaching & Projects Abroad,** Gerrard House, Rustington, West Sussex BN16 1AW. Tel: 01903 859911. Fax: 01903 785779. E-mail: info@teaching-abroad.co.uk Internet: www.teaching-abroad. co.uk

113 **Tearfund**, Transform Programme, 100 Church Road, Teddington, Middlesex TW11 8QE. Tel: 020 8943 7750. E-mail: transform@

tearfund.org Internet: www.tearfund.org/transform

TEFL Training, Friend's Close, Boot Street, Stonefield, Witney, Oxon OX8 8PX. Tel: 01993 891121. Fax: 01993 891686.

Terrance Higgins Trust Helpline, The, Tel: 020 7242 1010 (for advice and counselling on HIV/AIDS issues).

80 **Time For God (TFG)**, 7 Colney Hatch Lane, Muswell Hill, London N10 1PN. E-mail: Enquiry@timeforgod.org Internet: www. timeforgod.org

136 **Trailfinders**, 194 Kensington High Street, London W8 7RG, Tel: 020 7938 3939 *(longhaul travel)*, Tel: 020 77938 3444 *(visa & passport service)*, Tel: 020 7938 3999 *(travel clinic)*; 215 Kensington High Street, London W8 6BD (southside), Tel: 020 7937 5400 *(transatlantic & European travel)*; 42–50 Earls Court Road, London W8 6FT, Tel: 020 7938 3366 Fax: 020 7937 9294 *(longhaul travel)*, 020 7938 3858 *(groups of 10 or more)*, 1 Threadneedle Street, London EC2R 8JX. Tel: 020 7628 7628 *(worldwide)*; Tel: 020 7628 4567 *(visa & passport service)* ; 22–4 The Priory Queensway, Birmingham B4 6BS, Tel: 0121 236 1234 *(worldwide travel)*; 48 Corn Street, Bristol BS1 1HQ, Tel: 0117 929 9000 *(worldwide)*; 254 284 Sauchiehall Street, Glasgow G2 3EH, Tel: 0141 353 2224 *(worldwide)*; 58 Deansgate, Manchester M3 2FF, Tel: 0161 839 3434 *(worldwide)*; 7-9 Ridley Place, Newcastle-upon-Tyne NE1 8JQ. Tel: 0191 261 2345 *(worldwide)*; 4/5 Dawson Street, Dublin 2, Ireland. Tel: 00 353 1 677 7888 *(worldwide)*.

18 **Travel Companions**, 2 Coxhill Cottages, Boldre, Lymington, Hampshire SO41 8PS. Tel: 01590 683005. E-mail: coxhill@bt internet.com Internet: http://oasis.fortunecity.com/myrtle/330

176 **Trekforce Expeditions,** 34 Buckingham Palace Road, London SW1 0RE. Tel: 020 7828 2275. Fax: 020 7828 2276. E-mail: trekforce@dial.pipex.com Internet: www.trekforce.org.uk

7 **UCAS (Universities and Colleges Admissions Service),** Rosehill, New Barn Lane, Cheltenham, Gloucestershire GL52 3LZ. Tel: 01242 222444 (general enquiries) or 01242 227788 (applicant enquiries). Fax: 01242 221622. E-mail: enq@ucas.ac.uk Internet: www.ucas. ac.uk

94 **United Society for the Propagation of the Gospel** – see Experience Exchange Programme

136 **Usit Campus** , 52 Grosvenor Gardens, London SW1W 0AG. Tel:0870 240 1010 (national call centre). Fax: 020 7730 6893. *Manchester* Tel: 0161 273 1721; *Bristol* Tel: 0117 929 2494; *Scotland* Tel: 0131 668 3303. Internet: www.usitcampus.co.uk

56 **Verein für Internationale Jungendarbeit**, Goethestr. 10, 53225 Bonn, Germany. Tel: 49 228 69 89 52. Fax: 49 228 69 41 66.

57 **Visitoz Scheme, The**, 4C Queens Gate Place, London SW7 5NT. Tel: 020 7581 8627. E-mail: wdtb@aol.com Internet: www. visitoz.org

81 **Voluntary Service Belfast (VSB),** 70/72 Lisburn Road, Belfast BT9

6AF(Call in between 9am-5pm). Tel: 028 90 200850.
E-mail: info@vsb.org.uk. Internet: www.vsb.org.uk.

126 **Waterways Recovery Group (WRG)**, 114 Regent's Park Road,
London NW1 8UQ. Tel: 020 7586 2510. Internet: www.wrg.
org.uk

139 **West Dean College**, West Dean, Chichester, West Sussex PO18 0QZ.
Tel: 01243 811301. Fax: 01243 811343. E-mail: westdean@
pavilion.co.uk Internet: www.westdean.org.uk

177 **Wilderness Leadership School**, PO Box 53058. Yellowwood
Park 4011, Durban (mention contact through The Wilderness
Trust). Tel: 00 27 31 462 8642. Fax: 00 27 31 462 8675. E-mail:
wilderness.trails@eastcoast.co.za

177 **Wilderness Trust, The,** The Oast House, Hankham, nr Pevensey, East
Sussex BN24 5AP. Tel: 01323 461730. Fax: 01323 761913. E-mail:
wilderness.trust@dial.pipex Internet: www.wilderness trust.org

Winged Fellowship, Angel House, 20–32 Pentonville Road, London
N1 9XD. Tel: 020 7833 2594. Fax: 020 7278 0370.

139 **Workers' Educational Association**, Temple House, 17 Victoria Park
Square, London E2 9PB. Tel: 020 8983 1515. Fax: 020 8983 4840.
Internet: www.wea.org.uk

32 **World Challenge Expeditions**, Black Arrow House, 2 Chandos
Road, London NW10 6NF. Tel: 020 8728 7200. Fax: 020
8961 1551. E-mail: welcome@world-challenge.co.uk www.
world-challenge.co.uk

115 **World Exchange**, **Scottish Churches**, St Colm's International House,
23 Inverleith Terrace, Edinburgh EH3 5N3.

115 **World Horizons,** Centre for the Nations, North Dock, Llanelli, South
Wales SA15 2LF. Tel: 01554 750005. Fax: 01554 773304. E-mail:
ndock@whorizons.org   Internet: www.worldhorizons.
org

82 **World Service Enquiry/Christians Abroad**, Suite 233, Bon Marché
Centre, 241-251 Ferndale Road, London SW9 8BJ. *World Service
Enquiry* Tel: 0207 346 5950. Fax: 0207 346 5955. E-mail:
wse@cabroad.org.uk *Christians Abroad* Tel: 0207 346 5956. Fax:
0207 346 5955. E-mail: admin@cabroad.org.uk

World University Service (UK), 14 Dufferin Street, London EC1Y
8PD. Tel: 020 7426 5820. Fax: 020 7251 1315.

127 **WWOOF (Willing Workers on Organic Farms)**, PO Box 2675,
Lewes, East Sussex BN7 1RB. Internet: www.phdcc.com/wwoof

117 **Year for God**, Holmsted Manor, Staplefield Road, Cuckfield, West
Sussex RH17 5JF. Tel: 01444 443016. Fax: 01444 450770.
E-mail: YFG@holmsted.org.uk Internet: www.holmsted.org.uk

148 **Year in Industry, The**, National Director, University of Manchester,
Simon Building, Oxford Road, Manchester M13 9PL. Tel/Fax: 0161
275 4396. E-mail: enquires@yini.org.uk Internet: www.
yini.org.uk The Year in Industry is available through a network of
regional centres. Contact the address above for the details of your
nearest centre.

2   **Year Out Group, The,** PO Box 29925, London SW6 6FQ. Tel: 07980 395789. Internet: www.yearoutgroup.org

58   **Young Farmers' Clubs, National Federation of (YFC),** The International Farm Experience Programme, YFC Centre, National Agriculture Centre, Stoneleigh Park, Kenilworth, Warwickshire CV8 2LG. Tel: 01203 696544.

116   **Youth Action for Peace UK (YAP),** 8 Golden Ridge Freshwater, Isle of Wight 9040 9LE. Tel/fax: 01983 750069. E-mail: wnbeacon@lineone.net or rociogo@yahoo.com Internet: www.yap.org

153   **Youth Exchange Centre,** The British Council, 10 Spring Gardens, London SW1A 2BN. Tel: 020 7389 4030. Fax: 020 7389 4033. E-mail: yec.enquiries@britishcouncil.org Internet: www.youth org.uk/yec

83   **Youth For Britain,** Higher Orchard, Sandford Orcas, Sherborne, Dorset DT9 4RP. Tel/Fax: 01963 220 036. E-mail: yfb@world vol.co.uk

162   **Youth for Understanding UK,** Unit 1D3, Templeton Business Centre, Glasgow G40 1DA. Tel: 0141 556 1116. Fax: 0141 551 0949. E-mail: yfu@exchange18.freeserve.com Internet: www. youth-for-understanding.freeserve.co.uk

13,   **Youth Hostels Association (England and Wales) (YHA),**
119   Trevelyan House, 8 St Stephen's Hill, St Albans, Herts AL1 2DY. Tel: 01727 845 047. Fax: 01727 844126. E-mail: customerservices@yha.org.uk Internet: www.yha.org.uk ; *Hostel International Northern Ireland,* 22 Donegall Road, Belfast BT12 5JN. Tel: 01232 324733. Fax: 01232 439699. E-mail: info@hini.org.uk Internet: www.hini.org.uk ; *Scottish Youth Hostels Association,* 7 Glebe Crescent, Stirling FK8 2JA. Tel: 01786 891400. Fax: 01786 891333. E-mail: info@syha.org.uk Internet: www.syha.org.uk ; *Irish Youth Hostel Association (Anœige),* 61 Mountjoy Street, Dublin 7, Ireland. Tel: 353 1 830 4555. Fax: 353 1 830 5808. E-mail: anoige@iol.ie Internet: www.irelandyha.org